CW00555380

Endorsements

"Death is often frightening, and talking about death can feel awkward. But death is real, and we must face it as an inevitable reality for ourselves and others until the Lord returns. Furthermore, believers in Christ have victory over death and need not dread it. Guy Waters has written a biblically faithful, personally helpful, and radiantly hopeful book about death so that, by God's grace, we can be prepared to face death and to help others to do the same. Whether you are a pastor, counselor, caring friend, or just someone who wants to be ready to die with confident hope in the Lord, this book offers substantive answers to questions about our final destinies."

—Dr. Joel R. Beeke
President and professor of systematic theology and homiletics
Puritan Reformed Theological Seminary, Grand Rapids, Mich.

"In these pages, Guy Prentiss Waters takes us gently, but securely, by the hand, and leads us through twelve chapters of biblically rich, pastorally reliable, spiritually wise, and deeply sensitive teaching to help us overcome death and the fears that accompany it. *Facing the Last Enemy* simultaneously answers our questions and reassures us that if we can say with Paul 'to me to live is Christ' then we can also be confident that 'to die is gain.' It is a classic of its kind and deserves a place in every home."

—Dr. Sinclair B. Ferguson,
Teaching fellow
Ligonier Ministries

"As a society, we tend to avoid facing the reality of death, and as a result, we often find ourselves unprepared for it when it comes to us or to a loved one. Even Christians' views of dying and what happens next may be fuzzy. But the Bible offers *so much* help and hope in the face of death. The reality of who God is, His overarching plan, and how Jesus' resurrection transforms death for His people touches down in our lives with concrete hope that changes everything in the midst of heartbreak and loss. Waters has done a great service in presenting a thorough account of biblical truth about death, dying, and grief as well as insights and advice that are both pastoral and practical. You will find this a very helpful resource."

—Mrs. Elizabeth W.D. Groves
Lecturer in biblical Hebrew
Westminster Theological Seminary, Philadelphia

"In short order, Dr. Waters has provided for us a theologically sound and practical book on the matter that faces us all: our death and what happens afterwards. Written with the eye of a New Testament scholar, but accessible to everyone, *Facing the Last Enemy* will provide invaluable help to those facing death and their next of kin. I know nothing that meets this important need as well as this book does, and I will be highly recommending it at the church at which I serve. Invaluable."

—Dr. Derek W.H. Thomas
Senior minister,
First Presbyterian Church, Columbia, S.C.

"Having reached my allotted three score years and ten, I have been realizing that I need to face up to the reality of death. This book has helped me to do so, not in a morbid or fearful way but in the assurance provided by the life-giving Word of God. In his thorough treatment of what the Bible teaches about death in all its nuances, Guy Waters has written a book that will be invaluable for pastors, for those who grieve, and for the dying, which all of us are. *Facing the Last Enemy* consistently shows the connection between our death and the death of Christ, and His resurrection and our resurrection."

—Dr. Gene Edward Veith
Provost and professor emeritus
Patrick Henry College, Purcellville, Va.

Facing the Last Enemy

Facing the Last Enemy

Death and the Christian

GUY PRENTISS WATERS

 LIGONIER MINISTRIES

Facing the Last Enemy: Death and the Christian
© 2023 by Guy Prentiss Waters

Published by Ligonier Ministries
421 Ligonier Court, Sanford, FL 32771
Ligonier.org

Printed in China
Amity Printing Company
0000323
First printing

ISBN 978-1-64289-434-9 (Hardcover)
ISBN 978-1-64289-435-6 (ePub)

All rights reserved. No part of this publication may be reproduced, stored in a retrieval system, or transmitted in any form or by any means—electronic, mechanical, photocopy, recording, or otherwise—without the prior written permission of the publisher, Ligonier Ministries. The only exception is brief quotations in published reviews.

Cover design: Jessica Hiatt
Interior design and typeset: Katherine Lloyd, The DESK

Scripture quotations are from the ESV® Bible (The Holy Bible, English Standard Version®), copyright © 2001 by Crossway, a publishing ministry of Good News Publishers. Used by permission. All rights reserved.

Library of Congress Control Number: 2021952226

To

Will Thompson (1944–2021)

and

Becky Thompson

Contents

Acknowledgments xi

Part One: Defining Death

1   What Is Death? (Part 1) 3

2   What Is Death? (Part 2) 13

3   What Happens after Death? 23

4   Why Did Christ Die? 33

5   Why Do Christians Die? 43

Part Two: Encountering Death

6   How Do I Face the Deaths of Others? 57

7   How Do I Help the Dying and Grieving? 67

8   How Do I Prepare for Death? (Part 1) 79

9   How Do I Prepare for Death? (Part 2) 89

Part Three: Beyond Death

10   What Does the Bible Teach about the Resurrection? 101

11   What Does the Bible Teach about the Final Judgment? 113

12   What Does the Bible Teach about Heaven and Hell? 123

Notes 133

Subject Index 145

Scripture Index 151

About the Author 157

Acknowledgments

It is only fitting that I recognize my debts to a number of people without whom this book would not be in your hands. I have the privilege of serving as the James M. Baird Jr. Professor of New Testament at Reformed Theological Seminary in Jackson, Miss. The board of trustees graciously awarded me a sabbatical from December 2020 to August 2021, during which I drafted and edited the manuscript. I am grateful for all that they do—much of it unseen and all of it sacrificial—to enable me and my colleagues to take up the high calling of preparing generations of men and women for service in the kingdom of God.

I am thankful for my fellow faculty members and the administration of RTS. Their faithfulness to the Word of God and their love for Christ and His cause encourage me daily. In particular, Dr. Ligon Duncan, chancellor and chief executive officer of RTS; Dr. Robert Cara, chief academic officer; and Dr. Miles Van Pelt, academic dean, RTS Jackson, have extended support and encouragement to me in my service at RTS. I am grateful to God for their steadfast labors and their many years of friendship.

I am profoundly appreciative to my family for their continued love and care—my wife, Sarah, and my children, Phoebe, Lydia, and Thomas. Every day they point me to the Savior in gratitude for His many mercies.

I am thankful to friends and colleagues who read portions or even all of this book in manuscript form. The Rev. Nathan Lee, James O'Brien, and the Rev. Kevin Vollema read the entirety of the draft and offered careful, perceptive comments. The work is markedly stronger and clearer as a result of their editorial labors. Drs. Elizabeth and Sam Hensley—friends, theologians, and faithful Christian physicians—read chapter 9 and offered invaluable counsel and assistance. My Jackson colleague and friend the Rev. Dr. Bruce P. Baugus similarly read an early draft of a portion of chapter 9 and offered perceptive comment.

I am grateful to all at Ligonier who made it possible for this book to go to press. Particular thanks go to Rev. Joe Holland, Rev. Aaron L. Garriott, Rev. Thomas Brewer, Rev. Kevin D. Gardner, and Chris Larson. Their professionalism and grace have been extraordinary and have made this project a delight to undertake.

This book originated as a Sunday school series at the Second Presbyterian Church, Yazoo City, Miss., from November 2020 to April 2021. The congregation faithfully attended and offered thoughtful questions and insights, many of which have made their way into this book. Their love for the Word of God and devotion to Christ humble me and encourage me. It was my sheer privilege to open this portion of Scripture's teaching to them for those months.

The genesis of this project was a request from a friend and ruling elder at Second Presbyterian Church, Dr. William Puffer Thompson. Will wrote me in September 2020 as he was facing the end stages of cancer with a simple and powerful question: "How do I prepare to die?" The Sunday school series and this book were the fruits of that query. Will finished his earthly course and passed into glory on February 14, 2021, meeting face-to-face the Savior whom he had long loved and served. It is to him and to his faithful, godly widow, Rebecca (Becky) Allen Thompson, that this book is affectionately dedicated.

Part One

DEFINING DEATH

1

What Is Death?
(Part 1)

We all have questions about death. "What is death? Why do we die? Why do we all die? Why is death so scary? Why did Christ die? Why do Christians have to die? How can I face the death of someone I love? How can I prepare for death? How can I help others prepare for death? What happens after death?"

To answer these questions, we need to go to Scripture and see what God has to say to us there. The Bible is God's Word and is completely reliable and true. If the Bible tells us something about death, then we can stake our lives on it.

We also have a lot of help. Our spiritual ancestors thought deeply and practically about death. Throughout church history, pastors and teachers have sought to help God's people face death in light of the riches of biblical truth. With the Protestant Reformation five centuries ago, the church recovered the gospel in its full biblical integrity. Martin Luther, John Calvin, the British Puritans, and their spiritual heirs have left us rich reflections on suffering, death, and heaven in light of the gospel.

But we don't live in the halls of church history. We live in the twenty-first century. Every generation faces its own particular challenges in thinking seriously and biblically about death and dying. The challenges of the sixteenth and seventeenth centuries are not always our own. To begin, we need to think about where we are. Why does modern Western culture—and, sadly, sometimes even the church—make it so hard for us to think about death?

Challenges from Our Culture

What are some obstacles that our culture raises to thinking properly about death and dying? There are at least two. The first is that we live in a *culture of distraction*. Think about it. We have year-round access to sports—live and televised events, both domestic and international, including football, baseball, basketball, hockey, and soccer. We have cable networks, talk shows, call-in shows—all devoted to sports. We have television and movie streaming—Netflix, Hulu, Amazon Prime, Disney+, Apple TV, for starters. In 2019, 532 original scripted television series were broadcast in the United States, up from 495 in 2018 and 210 in 2009.[1] And then there are the twenty-four-hour news channels. You couldn't begin to watch all that's on offer. There is music streaming—Spotify, Pandora, Apple Music, Amazon Music. For a few dollars a month, you can stream or download hundreds or thousands of songs. And although social media is a relative newcomer, Facebook, Twitter, Instagram, Snapchat, and TikTok entice users to spend hours on their devices.

The point is not that sports, television, music, and social media are bad. They are not. I enjoy each of them. The problem is that our culture overwhelms us with entertainments and diversions. This multibillion-dollar industry entices us not to think about serious things—life, death, and eternity. Of course, diversion from serious things is not unique to our culture. It is part of our fallen bent as sinners to distract ourselves from the truth. Why do we do this? Blaise Pascal put it well nearly four hundred years ago: "Being unable to cure death, wretchedness and ignorance, men have decided, in order to be happy, not to think about such things"[2] and "It is easier to bear death when one is not thinking about it than the idea of death when there is no danger."[3]

Therefore, our culture has not done something brand-new in its pursuit of distraction. What is new is that we have taken distraction to new heights. The thought of death is so overwhelming that we would prefer not to think about it at all. Our modern industry of distraction helps us to do just that. We invest billions of dollars annually *not* to think about the unthinkable.

A second and related obstacle that our culture has raised to thinking seriously about death and dying is that we live in a *culture of distancing and denial*. We have all sorts of ways to try to keep death at arm's length. Few young people, for instance, have had direct experience with death. They see dramatizations of death on TV and in movies, often in shocking and gory detail.[4]

But many have never been to a funeral or memorial service, and even fewer have ever seen a dead body. It used to be that most people died at home. Now, most people die in institutions—hospitals and nursing homes, for instance.[5] This is not a bad thing, of course, since these institutions are routinely staffed by skilled people who ensure that our friends and family members receive care and comfort in their last days. But this also means that families are often not with their loved ones in their last hours. Further, a once-common experience of death in families has been mercifully stemmed—infant mortality. Parents, of course, continue to experience the tragic heartache of the loss of a child, but this is far less frequent than it used to be.[6] The eighteenth-century Scottish pastor Thomas Boston buried six children before they reached the age of two. The English Puritan John Owen had eleven children, but only one survived to adulthood. No one would want to return to the days when infant mortality was an expected, if not inevitable, part of family life. But that also means that fewer families today know what it is to experience death firsthand in the home.

We have also witnessed a revolution in the way that people mourn in our culture. Increasingly, funerals are called *celebrations of life*. This way of speaking serves to distance both the service and the mourners from the reality of death. One survey from 2019 found that the three most popular songs performed at funerals in the United Kingdom were Frank Sinatra's "My Way," Andrea Boccelli's "Time to Say Goodbye," and Eva Cassidy's recording of "Over the Rainbow."[7] It is revealing that these songs equip us to respond to death with sloppy sentimentality ("Time to Say Goodbye," "Over the Rainbow") or with bald defiance ("My Way"). The survey's authors commented that "surprisingly no classical hymns made it on to the most popular top ten list." Is this a surprise, though? Good hymns capture deep, substantive, biblical truths to bring gospel comfort to mourners. By and large, that is simply not what we want in the West today as we encounter death.

Challenges from the Church

The culture is not the only place where we find obstacles to thinking seriously and substantively about death and dying. Sadly, the evangelical church has added its own set of obstacles. We may briefly reflect on three in particular. First, the church has embraced *consumerism*. The church too often treats attenders like customers, who too often act like customers. The church can present itself as selling a product in a competitive marketplace. Church attenders can demand to be kept satisfied or they will take their business elsewhere. If that model informs, even imperceptibly, our understanding of the church, then mortality and death will struggle to find a place in the church's teaching and songs. If people are not made to feel positive and uplifted, the reasoning goes, they will leave and go elsewhere. There are incredible pressures to keep people coming and to attract more people to our services and programs. Why, then, would you put an unwelcome reality such as death before them?

Second, the church has embraced *an entertainment mentality*. Often the buildings in which evangelical churches meet resemble stages with auditorium-style seating. A band is up front, playing loud music (some churches even offer earplugs to attendees as they enter the building). Preaching reflects the influence of entertainment culture. Preaching is dedicated less to opening and applying a text of Scripture than to addressing the felt needs and concerns of contemporary hearers. It avoids being either serious or confrontational, and it is not particularly authoritative. Death and eternity, if they are handled at all, are handled sparingly and gingerly.

Third, the church *divides itself* by age and stage. This is not sinful in itself. It is good that believers, especially in large churches, can find and enjoy fellowship with other believers who are of a similar age and in the same stage of life. The danger is that this arrangement can distort the ministry of the church. For one thing, teaching and ministry are often geared toward the perceived needs and concerns of the group—college students, newly married, new moms, parents of teenagers, and so on. For many such groups, death and dying will be low on the list of teaching priorities. Further, when people gather into groups by affinity, they can easily lose contact with believers in the same church who are different from them. In particular, they lose the benefit of ready access to older believers—believers who have buried a child or a spouse; believers who are facing a terminal diagnosis; believers who have spent a lifetime ministering to grieving and mourning people. As a result, a whole generation of Christians is deprived of witnessing the truth of Scripture exemplified and lived out in the lives of older Christians.

In chronicling these obstacles, in both the culture and the church, we are not saying that these challenges are the result of some widespread, hidden conspiracy on the part of a handful of leaders in each. Nor are we saying that true Christians are immune to any one of these influences. What we are saying is that we face powerful headwinds as we prepare to think about the inevitable—mortality and eternity. The first step in facing these headwinds is to recognize that they are there. They not only blow within the culture, but they have even made their way into the church. Our response is not to wax nostalgic for an earlier, supposedly better age (see Eccl. 7:10). Rather, mindful of the challenges that are before us, we should commit ourselves to an earnest and careful study of the Bible.

What Is the Truth about Death?

In light of what we have seen, we should be careful to take nothing for granted when it comes to death and dying. That is to say, we will need to test every belief and conviction against the testimony of Scripture. Only what is true will equip us to understand and face death in the way that God wants. So where can we begin as we think about the Bible's testimony to death and dying? We will begin ... at the beginning. The first three chapters of the Bible, in fact, give us a wealth of information about life and death. We may look at five points in particular that Genesis 1–3 raises.

Death Is Not Part of the Original Creation

First, the Bible makes it clear that God does not build human death into the original creation. Genesis opens with the words "In the beginning, God..." (Gen. 1:1). Before the world was, there was only God. And God is the living and the true God, in whom there is no death or dying. He is life itself.

God, and God alone, makes the world *ex nihilo*, out of nothing (Gen. 1:1b; Heb. 11:3). When God creates the world, He both forms and fills— He creates habitations and sets "living creatures" in them (Gen. 1:20–21, 24). These living creatures are, in turn, commanded to be "fruitful and multiply" (v. 22). Living creatures model themselves after their Creator by bringing life into the world.

And then God creates man, the crown of creation, the only creature who is said to be made "in our image, after our likeness" (Gen. 1:26). The image of the living God presides over the life of the creation ("let them have

7

dominion"). Men and women likewise must be "fruitful and multiply and fill the earth and subdue it" (v. 28).

When God finishes making the world in the space of six days, He reviews the whole of His handiwork with complete satisfaction: "And behold, it was very good" (Gen. 1:31). The living God makes a world that is teeming with life and suited to promoting the life of His creatures. His creatures are endowed with the potential to produce more life. This includes human beings. All this is good. There is no hint whatsoever from the original creation that humans will die.

God Created Man a Living Being, Body and Soul

Second, Scripture tells us that God specially created man. We read a detailed description of Adam's creation in Genesis 2:7: "Then the LORD God formed the man of dust from the ground and breathed into his nostrils the breath of life, and the man became a living creature." God shows us something important about our humanity. God made Adam in two stages, reflecting the two constitutive parts of man. First, there is Adam's body. Adam's body was formed immediately by God from the dust of the earth. Second, there is Adam's soul. Adam's soul was formed when God "breathed into his nostrils the breath of life." Only when soul and body are joined together (and not before) does Adam become a "living creature." We may fairly infer that if a person's soul and body were ever to be separated, that person would cease to be a living creature. But there is no hint of death or of the principle of death in man as God creates him in Genesis 1–2. God created us, body and soul, to be living creatures in fellowship with Him and to serve Him on this earth.

Death Is the Penalty of Sin

Third, before sin enters the world, God gives Adam a warning in the garden of Eden: "You may surely eat of every tree of the garden, but of the tree of the knowledge of good and evil you shall not eat, for in the day that you eat of it you shall surely die" (Gen. 2:16–17). It is important to remember that God speaks these words to Adam before he sins or is even tempted to sin. Even before Adam's fall into sin, then, Adam had some idea or notion of what death was. To die is to be deprived of life, to lose the life that Adam had. Death, furthermore, was the penalty for disobeying God's command. Death, in the words of the Apostle, is "the wages of sin" (Rom. 6:23). Consequently, after Adam sins, God tells him that the threatened penalty will surely come upon him: "By the sweat of your face you shall eat bread, till you return to the ground, for out of it you were taken; for you are dust, and to dust you shall return" (Gen. 3:19). God's words make it clear that death for Adam will be the separation of his body and soul, and the return of his body whence it came— the dust of the ground.

Death is not, as so many understand it, a natural part of the cycle of life and existence. It is not built into our humanity. "Death is not a debt to nature, but is God's judgment upon sin."[8] Had sin not entered the world, death would have remained an abstract idea to human beings.

Death Is Universal in Its Scope

Fourth, death is universal in its scope. Experience tells us that all people will die. So does Scripture: "it is appointed for man to die once" (Heb. 9:27). This is graphically demonstrated in the genealogy of Genesis 5, just a couple of chapters after Adam's fall into sin. Early in the chapter we read, "Thus all the days that Adam lived were 930 years, and he died" (v. 5). The phrase "and he died" becomes a lamentable refrain throughout the chapter. All of Adam's listed descendants die. The one exception in Genesis 5 proves the rule: "Enoch walked with God, and he was not, for God took him" (v. 24). Enoch does not experience death, but God removes him all the same from the face of the earth.[9]

Scripture is plain: no one escapes death.[10] Neither rich nor poor. Neither powerful nor downtrodden. Neither beautiful nor ugly. Neither strong nor weak. Neither pious nor wicked. Death strikes at all ages and stages of life— the aged, people in their prime, youths, infants, even children in the womb. There are, of course, all the precursors to death that afflict people in this life— disease, injury, illness, bodily weakness, mental decay. These are not merely "part of living" or "growing old" but hints and harbingers of death.

Why is it that all die? We will explore this question further in the chapters ahead. For now, it is enough to say that if all die, then it is because all have sinned (see Rom. 5:12b). God is a just God. Death is the penalty of sin. God would not inflict death for no reason at all. He does not treat the innocent as though they were guilty. The universal reign of death testifies to the universal reach of sin in humanity.

Death Is Cosmic in Its Reach

Fifth, death is cosmic in its reach. We often think of death in terms of individual human beings. And that, of course, is right. But the Bible tells us that accompanying the infliction of death as the penalty for sin is the curse of God on the creation. Listen to what God tells Adam after Adam has sinned against God: "Cursed is the ground because of you; in pain you shall eat of it all the days of your life; thorns and thistles it shall bring forth for you; and you shall eat the plants of the field" (Gen. 3:17–18). The world will continue on, and Adam will continue to work the ground, just as God had commanded him at his creation. From now on, however, the world lies under God's curse. It will be marked and marred by frustration, pain, suffering, and death. The Apostle Paul gives eloquent testimony to this sad reality:

> For the creation was subjected to futility, not willingly, but because of him who subjected it, in hope that the creation itself will be set free from its bondage to corruption and obtain the freedom of the glory of the children of God. For we know that the whole creation has been groaning together in the pains of childbirth until now. (Rom. 8:20–22)

The creation did not, as it were, ask God to be the way that it now is. It has been brought into "bondage to corruption" and has been "subjected to futility." Animals suffer and die violent deaths. Earthquakes, wildfires, and hurricanes ravage the landscape. With one voice, then, the creation "groans together." But that groan accompanies the "pains of childbirth." This points to a greater, blessed reality that lies ahead—new heavens and a new earth. For the present, the creation is enslaved to decay and futility as the result of the entrance of sin, and with it death, into the world through Adam.

Conclusion

It is never pleasant to think about death. Yet death is real. It is not something that we can afford to ignore, to wish away, to sentimentalize, or to trivialize. Scripture owns up to the reality of death and does so from its opening pages. Issues of "life and death" importance mark the first three chapters of the Bible. If God wants us to think about death, then what does He want us to know? In the first place, death is loss. It is something to grieve and lament. It is not the way things are supposed to be. Therefore, it is the "last enemy" (1 Cor. 15:26). It is right to weep in the face of death.

Death is even worse than we may have imagined it to be. It is the penalty for sin. In chapter 3, we will see what happens when people die—they immediately enter the presence of their Creator and Judge. For sinners, this is bad news. The loss that death brings to everyone, however great, pales in comparison with what awaits those who die as God's enemies—eternal punishment and misery (what the Bible calls the "second death," Rev. 20:14).

There is, however, good news. God does not reveal these things to taunt or torment us. He reveals them to help us grasp our need for the Savior, whom the gospel offers to all sinners. Christ came into this world to live, die, and rise again for sinners. He has "taste[d] death for everyone" (Heb. 2:9), so He knows what it is to face death and experience death. But He does more than sympathize with us in the hour of death. He has conquered death. He has "abolished death and brought life and immortality to light through the gospel" (2 Tim. 1:10). "Through death he ... destroy[ed] the one who has the power of death, that is, the devil" (Heb. 2:14). He died on the cross and was raised from the grave for sinners and their salvation. This victory belongs to all those (and only to those) who put their trust in Him.

If we trust Christ, the "Author of life" (Acts 3:15), then we have the sure hope of eternal life. Death may lie ahead of us, but in God's hands death brings us into the fullness of eternal life. There, death will be only the stuff of memory: "And the ransomed of the LORD shall return and come to Zion with singing; everlasting joy shall be upon their heads; they shall obtain gladness and joy, and sorrow and sighing shall flee away" (Isa. 51:11). In glory, "God will wipe away every tear from [our] eyes" (Rev. 7:17). So we may weep in the days of our pilgrimage, but the day will come for us when tears of sorrow will give way to tears of joy. As Samuel Rutherford reminds us, "it were a well-spent journey, though sev'n deaths lay between ..., and glory, glory dwelleth in Emmanuel's land."[11]

2

What Is Death?
(Part 2)

I n the first chapter, we began to look at what the Bible teaches about death and dying. The Bible addresses issues of life and death at the very beginning—Genesis 1–3. In this chapter, we are going to build on that testimony. We will explore what Scripture tells us about the many dimensions of death, the certainty of death, and the fear that comes with death.

The Dimensions of Death

What do we mean by the *dimensions* of death? When we think of death, we typically think of a friend's or a loved one's dying. Certainly, the Bible speaks of death that way. The Bible also has a broader understanding of death than *biological* or *natural* death. It can speak of death in terms of a person's relationship with God. We may call this *spiritual* death. Third, the Bible understands death in its fullest dimension in light of eternity. Those who die impenitent enter *eternal* death. These three dimensions are not separate from one another. They are very much interrelated. Let's look at these three dimensions of death—biological, spiritual, and eternal.

Biological, or natural, death is the kind of death that is most familiar to us.[1] This death is the temporary dissolution of the bond between a person's soul and body. As a result, the body undergoes corruption. This is how Solomon speaks of death in Ecclesiastes 12:7: "The dust returns to the earth as it was, and the spirit returns to God who gave it." Compare Elihu's words: "If [God] should set his heart to it and gather to himself his spirit and his breath, all flesh would perish together, and man would return to dust" (Job 34:14–15). God had threatened Adam after he sinned: "You [will] return to the ground, for out of it you were taken; for you are dust, and to dust you shall return" (Gen. 3:19). Ecclesiastes reminds us that death is not the end of the soul's existence. The soul is not annihilated at death. On the contrary, at the moment of death the soul goes into the presence of its Creator. To begin to understand what happens at that meeting of the soul and its God, we need to think about the two other biblical dimensions of death.

The second dimension of death is spiritual death. There is a sense, according to Scripture, in which every person outside Jesus Christ is already dead. That is to say, death takes a grip on a person's life in the here and now, before that person's decease. Paul describes unbelieving people as "dead in . . . trespasses and sins" (Eph. 2:1; compare Col. 2:13). Paul can describe to Timothy an ungodly widow as "dead even while she lives" (1 Tim. 5:6).

This kind of death is not biological but relates to our disposition toward God. Those who are "dead" in this sense "walk" in the "trespasses and sins" that characterize their spiritual death (Eph. 2:1–2). Whereas the bodies of those who have died a natural death are inactive, spiritual death is quite active—in rebellion against and disobedience to God. In the verses that follow, Paul describes believers' former existence in spiritual death along three lines—the world, the devil, and the flesh. First, we once "follow[ed] the course of this world"—that is, we went along with the solidarity of human beings in rebellion against God (v. 2). Second, we once "follow[ed] the prince of the power of the air, the spirit that is now at work in the sons of disobedience" (v. 2). The devil and his demonic followers are active—invisibly but truly—to entice and to encourage sinners to live up to their name, "sons of disobedience." Third, we once "lived in the passions of our flesh, carrying out the desires of the body and the mind" (v. 3). "Flesh," for Paul, here describes our fallen humanity, bound over to the service of sin. Sin had complete mastery of our whole person, "body" and "mind."

We see evidence of spiritual death in the garden immediately after Eve and Adam fell into sin. Our first parents had been in fellowship with God, hearing and responding to His word (see Gen. 2:15–16; 3:8a). But once they sinned against God, what did they do? First, they covered themselves with fig leaves that they had sewn together (3:7). Then they "hid themselves from the presence of the LORD God among the trees of the garden" (v. 8b). The response of sinners to the presence of God is to cover and hide. Spiritual death, then, is a *running away* from God and a *running into* sin, with the encouragement and support of others and of Satan.

The third dimension of the Bible's testimony to death is eternal death. This dimension follows on from biological and spiritual death. Biological death is not the cessation of our existence. The soul is forcibly separated from the body and goes immediately into the presence of God. If a person dies outside Jesus Christ, then that person dies in a state of rebellion and hostility toward God. Death does not change that reality. The person enters God's presence as His enemy, justly deserving His punishment. The Bible uses the word "death" to describe that person's condition in eternity. In Revelation, John speaks of "the second death," which has no power over believers but is the condition of unbelievers in eternity (Rev. 20:6). A few verses later, John connects "the second death" with "the lake of fire," the place of the eternal torment of the wicked and of the devil (20:14; see also 20:10). In "hell," the impenitent will suffer in their whole person, "both soul and body" (Matt. 10:28).[2]

God's punishments do not change the heart (see Rev. 16:10–11). If a person enters eternity as the enemy of God, nothing will change that. This person loves sin and hates God. God's majesty and splendor, God's punishment and wrath will not change his heart. Therefore, God justly judges and punishes him, forever. This helps us understand why Jesus speaks of that punishment as "eternal punishment" (Matt. 25:46; compare Dan. 12:2).

There are, then, three interrelated dimensions of death. Biological death describes the separation of the soul from the body, the entrance of the soul into the presence of God, and the dissolution of the body into the dust of the ground. Spiritual death relates to the deadness of sinners in their sins. They are sinners from conception. Dead toward God, they are most active in their sinning. Every additional sin they commit merits "death" from God (Rom. 6:23). Eternal death is the ultimate dimension of death in Scripture. It describes the eternal condition of unreconciled sinners. It is a state of eternal punishment by a just God. Sadly, the justice of God and the punishment of the sinner will not break his love for sin or bring him to love God. That is one important reason that we may speak of death in this sense as *eternal*.

The Certainty of Death

Many of us are familiar with Benjamin Franklin's quote: "In this world nothing can be said to be certain, except death and taxes." Certainly, experience testifies that all people will die. Scripture confirms this testimony. The author of the epistle to the Hebrews tells us that "it is appointed for man to die once" (Heb. 9:27). All humans will die. No one escapes death. This is not accidental. It is a matter of God's decree ("it is appointed"). God has decreed that all people will die. That decree is fixed and unchangeable. God is not passive in the execution of His decree; Moses writes, "You return man to dust and say, 'Return, O children of man!'" (Ps. 90:3).

God has also appointed the exact day and time of a person's death. In Psalm 139:16, David acknowledges to God, "In your book were written, every one of them, the days that were formed for me, when as yet there was none of them." Every one of our days, from first to last, has been eternally appointed by God. For that reason, our life and death are entirely subject to God's will. James tells us: "Come now, you who say, 'Today or tomorrow we will go into such and such a town and spend a year there and trade and make a profit'—yet you do not know what tomorrow will bring. What is your life? For you are a mist that appears for a little time and then vanishes. Instead you ought to say, 'If the Lord wills, we will live and do this or that'" (James 4:13–15). James' point is clear. Life is short and transient. We have no say or control over the length of our days—whether we will be alive tomorrow or not. The end of our days is set by the Lord's will. We need to live mindful of that reality. The rich fool of Jesus' parable is a fool because he lives as though he has many days to pursue his selfish pleasure. "But God said to him, 'Fool! This night your soul is required of you'" (Luke 12:20). The wise person is the one who knows that the length of his days is fixed by the decree of God and lives in light of that reality. This is why Moses instructs us to pray, "Teach us to number our days" (Ps. 90:12).

So death is certain to come to all, and it comes to each person at the exact time that God has eternally appointed it to come. That raises the question, Why? Why is it that all people die, without exception? Young, old; rich, poor; men, women; virtuous, wicked; devout, irreligious—all people die sometime.

God is a just God. He is not arbitrary or capricious. He always acts according to His own just and righteous character. If all people die, and all people die according to God's eternal and unchangeable purpose, then God must have a righteous reason for purposing their deaths.

We will be answering this question over the next few chapters. We may start with Paul's words to the Corinthians: "In Adam all die" (1 Cor. 15:22). Adam sinned and died; we sin and die. What is the connection between Adam's sin and death and our sin and death? Romans 5:12–21 helps us understand that connection.[3] In those verses, Paul tells us that God established a representative relationship between Adam and all human beings descending from him by ordinary generation (see Westminster Confession of Faith 6.3).[4] Adam stands as the representative of every human being (Jesus excepted). When Adam sinned, Paul reasons, he sinned not as a private person but as the representative of multitudes of human beings. Adam's sin is imputed (credited, transferred) to all those people whom he represents. In God's courtroom, Adam's sin is our sin. We have legal responsibility for that sin. We are liable to God's justice for that sin. Therefore, we die—Adam sinned and died; we are in Adam; therefore, Adam's sin is our sin, and Adam's death penalty is our death penalty.

You may pause at this point. "I thought you said that God is just in everything He does. But this seems unjust. Why am I being punished for something that someone else did? I didn't ask to be in Adam, and I didn't ask for Adam's sin. Why should I die?"

God is in fact just in everything that He does. His justice (as well as His goodness) shines forth in the covenantal relationship that He established between Adam and human beings. We may see this along five lines.

First, we need to remember that we are God's creatures. He has made us. We did not make ourselves. He has full rights to do with us as He pleases (Rom. 9:20–21). If He wants to establish a representative relationship among human beings, that is His sovereign prerogative (He didn't do this with the angels). Note as well that our representative, Adam, was created righteous, without sin. He is just the sort of representative whom we would have chosen ourselves. There is therefore nothing at all unjust about God's setting up this relationship within humanity at the creation.

Second, we should remember that we have many examples of representative relationships in daily life. For example, those of us who live under democratically elected governments often elect officials who represent us (and all their other constituents) in regional or national legislatures. I have a state representative and a state senator who represent me in Jackson, Miss. I have a congressman and two senators who represent me in Washington, D.C. What my state legislature or the U.S. Congress does is the action of the entire state or the nation. If Congress declares war against another country, then I and my fellow citizens have acted through our elected representatives. This is not a perfect analogy, of course, but it is one illustration of how the action of a few justly becomes the action of the many. Under Adam, the action of the one man, Adam, was credited to the many—all the people whom Adam represents.

Third, we should remember that God's intentions in the garden were only good. God set Adam in Paradise, surrounded by plenty. Adam was already in fellowship with God, who was near him and who spoke to him. When God threatened "death" to Adam for sinning, He was also offering him "life" for continuing in obedience to Him—confirmed, heightened, eternal life and fellowship with the triune God. And all Adam had to do was not to eat fruit from a single tree (among many). If Adam had done that, then all humanity would have benefited from the reward of Adam's obedience—everlasting life and fellowship with God. The whole arrangement is stamped with the generosity and kindness of a good God.

Fourth, if we insist on objecting to the justice of God in establishing this relationship between Adam and human beings, thereby holding us accountable for Adam's action, then we need to pause and examine ourselves. Our actions speak far louder than our words. If we are sinners by nature, then we love to sin. How can we protest this arrangement when, every day, we show both our love and preference for sin? Surely our protests ring hollow.

Fifth, to look at what Paul says about Adam in Romans 5:12–21 (or 1 Cor. 15, for that matter) is to see only half the story. Paul is not telling us only about Adam. He is comparing the person and disobedience of Adam with the person and obedience of Christ. Paul is helping us to see the gracious depths of the gospel. In mercy, God unites sinners to Christ. Christ stands as their representative before God. Their disobedience is counted to Him at the cross. That is why He dies an accursed death on the cross (see Deut. 21:22–23; 2 Cor. 5:21; Gal. 3:10, 13). But Christ's life of perfect obedience and His sacrificial death for sin are counted to sinners the moment they put their trust in Christ as He is offered in the gospel. This transfer of "righteousness" is the free gift of God. No sinner deserves it. God treats sinners in His courtroom in just the same way that He treats His glorified Son. Because of our sin, Jesus was treated as a sinner. Because of Jesus' obedience, we are treated as righteous. We get the life and glory that Jesus earned for us.

None of this, of course, is "fair"—God is not treating us the way that we deserve. Sinners really don't want *fairness* from God. That is to say, if God dealt with us fairly—according to our own record—then we would all perish (see Ps. 130:3). As sinners, we should want *mercy* from God. We really don't want from God what we deserve. We really don't want to stand on our own before a righteous, holy, all-seeing, and all-powerful God. We should want to stand on the work of another, the work of the God-man, Jesus Christ. That is exactly what God is pleased to give in the gospel. Our life and destiny are not earned by anything that we have done, are doing, or ever will do. Salvation has been finally and unchangeably earned by the work of Christ, which the Father has accepted and in which the Father takes unspeakable delight. It is graciously given to all who come to Christ. Even to be able to receive the work of Jesus for life and salvation is the free gift of God (see Eph. 2:8; Phil. 1:29). Salvation is all of grace, from start to finish. No one can boast in the presence of God. The one who understands his sins and who understands what Christ has done for sinners would have it no other way.

The Fear of Death

Death is a certainty, and death also inspires fear and dread in the hearts of human beings. As I write, the COVID-19 pandemic that spread across the globe in 2020 is responsible for the loss of millions of lives. Death has become real and palpable to many people in ways that it was not before the pandemic. The response, to put it mildly, has not been one of joy and serenity. People are afraid, and the possibility of death is no small part of that fear.

This reality raises two questions. First, is death a genuinely fearful thing? Second, if it is, why is that the case? The answer to the first question is yes, death is a genuinely fearful thing in itself, especially to human beings who are estranged from God and unreconciled to Him.[5] Hebrews powerfully testifies to the fear that death brings to human beings. Sinners are held in "lifelong slavery" because of the "fear of death" (Heb. 2:15). Satan holds the "power of death" insofar as he tempts people to sin, accuses sinners of their sins, and, in God's providence, wields a certain power over death (v. 14). Sinners are powerless to free themselves from the enslavement of the fear of death and from the vise grip of the power of death. That bondage can be broken in only one way—through the death of the incarnate Son of God (v. 14).

This fear of death helps to account for the world's strategy of distraction and diversion that we considered in the first chapter. Death is something that is intolerable to think about. Yet death is real and cannot be avoided, so the world flees to a refuge from despair—"We can't make it go away, so let's try not to think about it." Distract the mind. Divert the mind. Don't think on matters of eternal consequence. The shadow or pall that death casts on fallen humanity prompts our second question. Why does death inspire fear in the minds and hearts of people? We can identify at least three reasons that that is so.

First, while the day and hour of one's death is fixed by the eternal counsel of God, it is unrevealed to human beings. What Paul says of the suddenness of the arrival of the day of judgment is true of the arrival of our own death—it comes upon us "like a thief in the night," "as labor pains come upon a pregnant woman" (1 Thess. 5:2–3). In other words, it comes unannounced. The unwelcome and unpleasant certainty of death strikes us in a time, place, and manner that we (usually) don't know in advance. From our perspective, it can seem random and unpredictable. More than that, death is final. No one ever returns from death to life. Death ends our present form of existence—the life we have on this earth—in every real sense of the word.

Second, not only is death fixed and final, but it is also loss. Death deprives us of what is familiar and dear to us. Death takes from us our family and friends, our jobs and hobbies, our pursuits and ambitions. In the words of Job: "Naked I came from my mother's womb, and naked shall I return. The LORD gave, and the LORD has taken away" (Job 1:21; compare Ps. 49:17). The English Puritan William Bates puts it graphically: "There is a natural love of society in man, and death removes from all. The grave is a frightful solitude. . . . Every one among the dead is confined to his sealed, obscure cell, and is alone an entertainment for the worms."[6]

Death is loss in an even more profound sense. Death ruptures the bond between a person's soul and body. Paul describes this condition as being "naked" or "unclothed" (2 Cor. 5:3–4). God created us body and soul. The severance of that bond touches us at the core of what we are as human beings.[7]

Third, death is penal. This is the deepest reason that death inspires fear. Death comes as the penalty for sin. It is inflicted by a God who is just, righteous, and holy. Whether death is prolonged or instant, full of pain or free of pain, death ushers us into the presence of God. In that sense, death is like a warrant issued for a person's arrest. That person will be brought before the bar of justice to give an account of himself. In the same way, death is God's summons to bring a human being into His presence that he may give to God an account of himself. That is why Hebrews reminds us that "it is a fearful thing to fall into the hands of the living God" (Heb. 10:31).[8]

Conclusion

The matters that we have raised in this chapter are difficult, but they are matters that we have to face. We have to face them because they are true, revealed in the Word of God to human beings, and affecting the life and destiny of every human being. One thing that we have seen is that no one can truly understand death without first understanding God. The inescapability of death reflects the fact that we are, by nature, "dead in . . . trespasses and sins" (Eph. 2:1)—in rebellion against the living God. The time and circumstances of one's death have been fixed by the eternal, unchangeable decree of God. Death is not a biological inevitability or the turning of the wheels of a mechanical and impersonal universe. It is the penalty inflicted by a just, personal God. Death is fearful for just that reason—it is the punishment for sin. Death is not good and can never be enjoyable or desirable in itself.

As believers, we should view death as an opportunity to encourage people to think about God, eternity, and themselves in a biblical way (see Eccl. 7:2). If death is a raw wound, then only the medicine of the gospel will bring true and lasting healing. Death exposes the vanity and futility of people who try to live without God and to live for the pursuit of self and pleasure. Death intrudes and gives the lie to such a mindset and lifestyle. Are we ready to speak a good word to someone whose life has been turned upside down by the death of a loved one or the news of his own impending death? Are we prepared to help him understand it and to point him to the Savior, who conquered death?

What difference does being a Christian make to the reality and experience of death? That will be the focus of the chapters ahead. For now, we can say that while death is not good in itself, for those who are in Christ, death will be *for* our good. For His people, Christ brings an end not to the *experience* of death but to the *fear* of death. That is to say, death and its terrors no longer hold us in bondage. Why is that? Because Christ died, experiencing death in all its terrors, pains, horrors, and agonies of soul and body. Because Christ, in His death and resurrection, defeated death. He did this for us. As we approach death, we need to see it through the spectacles of the finished work of Christ. The gospel tells us that Christ has conquered and subdued death. That is the only way that we can face death with hope or confidence.

Only in Christ can we say, with Paul, "For to me to live is Christ, and to die is gain" (Phil. 1:21). Notice that only those who can say "for to me to live is Christ" can say "to die is gain." When we are brought from Adam to Christ, we exchange death for life, condemnation for justification (Rom. 8:1). If you are in Christ, then His obedience and death belong to you. You are counted righteous in Christ through faith alone, apart from anything that you have done, are doing, or ever will do (3:21–26). This gift of imputed righteousness gives you a lasting title to life and glory (5:17, 21).

The gospel completely changes our anticipation and experience of death. While the time and circumstances of our death are uncertain to us, we know that they have been eternally fixed by our heavenly Father. Our Father, who wants nothing for us but what is for our everlasting good, has appointed those details in His love and wisdom. Death is loss, in some important senses, but it is greater gain. Death ushers us into the riches of heaven and glory. When death brings us into the presence of God, we approach One who is our friend, One who welcomes us with open arms, One who delights in our presence with Him. The God whom we know and love here on earth is the God whose presence we will enjoy more fully in heaven above. In fellowship with God, there is no death, only life!

3

What Happens after Death?

We now have a basic idea of what the Bible means when it speaks of death. As we saw earlier, the Bible's opening pages speak of matters of life and death. The whole of Scripture helps us to understand death in all its dimensions, the certainty of death, and the fear and dread that death can prompt.

What happens after a person dies? Where do people go? What is their fate? These are questions that most people have thought about at some point in their lives. Philosophers, poets, and sages have applied themselves to these questions. How does the Bible answer them? How does the Bible help us think about what theologians call the *intermediate state*, the period between a person's death and the glorious return of Christ at the end of the age? Before we look at the teaching of the Bible, we need to think about four unbiblical understandings of what happens after death. These views have been promoted by learned theologians and have been embraced by people within the church. We will briefly describe each view and offer a biblical response.

What Doesn't Happen after Death?

Universalism

Universalism teaches that everyone will be saved. For this reason, universalism has an optimistic view of life after death—all people will enter an eternal state of happiness, peace, and joy. There are various forms of universalism. For some, everyone will be saved by following his own religion, whatever it may be. For others, everyone will ultimately be saved by the work of Christ.[1] The ground or reason offered for universal salvation is typically the love of God. If God is love, then love will prevail, and everyone will be saved.[2]

The Bible does speak of salvation as universal, but only in the sense that all kinds of people will be saved. No one is excluded from being saved because of gender, race, class, or any other such condition. This is the song of the saints in heaven as they praise Jesus Christ: "Worthy are you to take the scroll and to open its seals, for you were slain, and by your blood you ransomed people for God from every tribe and language and people and nation" (Rev. 5:9). But while the Bible teaches that salvation is *universal*, it does not teach *universalism*. We may see this along four lines.

First, the Bible teaches that all people are by nature "dead in . . . trespasses and sins" (Eph. 2:1). As Paul teaches elsewhere, "in Adam all die" (1 Cor. 15:22). We are conceived and born in sin and iniquity (see Ps. 51:5). From the moment of our conception, we are sinners by nature, enemies of God and of righteousness. Paul describes the (universal) human condition bleakly in Romans 1:18–32. A little later in that epistle, Paul quotes the Old Testament to underscore the native depravity of human beings: "No one understands; no one seeks for God. All have turned aside" (Rom. 3:11–12, quoting Ps. 14:1–3). Our minds are darkened, our wills turn away from God, and our affections are corrupted. This is why David declares, "God is angry with the wicked every day" (Ps. 7:11, KJV).

By nature, we are in a state of rebellion against God. Death does nothing to change that state. It has no power to make the wicked righteous or to make God's enemies His friends. We enter eternity as we exit from this life. Unless we are changed before death, we will enter eternity as God's enemies. The wrath of God that is now on display in this age (Rom. 1:18) is a harbinger of the wrath of the day of judgment (2:5).

Second, the Bible teaches that there is salvation and reconciliation in Christ alone and through faith in Him alone. The good news of the gospel is that there *is* salvation for sinners. And that salvation, the gospel stresses, is found only in union and communion with Jesus Christ, the last Adam (Rom. 5:12–21; 1 Cor. 15:22). Jesus Himself proclaimed: "I am the way, and the truth, and the life. No one comes to the Father except through me" (John 14:6). His Apostles testified, "And there is salvation in no one else, for there is no other name under heaven given among men by which we must be saved" (Acts 4:12), and "Whoever has the Son has life; whoever does not have the Son of God does not have life" (1 John 5:12). As John reminds us at the close of Jesus' exchange with Nicodemus in John 3:36, "Whoever believes in the Son has eternal life; whoever does not obey the Son shall not see life, but the wrath of God remains on him." The only way that one may flee the wrath to come and find eternal life is through faith in Christ.

Third, the window for salvation will not be open indefinitely. It will forever close when Christ returns in judgment. Paul reminds the Corinthians, "Behold, now is the favorable time; behold, now is the day of salvation" (2 Cor. 6:2). The "now" of which Paul speaks is the present age of redemptive history. It will close when Christ returns, as Paul teaches in 2 Thessalonians 1:5–12. Christ's first coming was an errand of salvation; Christ's second coming will be an errand of judgment.[3] His first appearing was in grace, to save. His second appearing will be in glory, to judge.

Fourth, when Christ returns to judge the world, His angels will gather all people, and all people will be separated into two groups, the righteous and the wicked. This is Jesus' teaching in His well-known parable of the sheep and the goats (Matt. 25:31–46). The wicked, after giving their account to Christ their Judge, will "go away into eternal punishment" (v. 46). This punishment is not therapeutic or remedial. It is not designed to save them in any way. It is judicial and penal (Rev. 14:9–11).

"But what about the love of God?" someone may object. How can we reconcile God's condemnation and eternal punishment of human beings with His love? How can a loving God send people to hell?

In answering this question, it is important that we not isolate one attribute of God (His love) from His other attributes (His justice, righteousness, and holiness). Nor must we ever pit one attribute of God against any other. All of God's attributes exist in perfect unity and harmony. The God who is love is the God who is holy and righteous.

We must also remember that there are no innocent people in hell. God has not dealt unjustly with a single one of them. They are being justly punished for their sins. Each has chosen rebellion against the God whom they know from the whole of the creation (Rom. 1:20–21). Some have further rebelled against God by refusing the offer of His Son to them for salvation (2 Thess. 1:8). All are being punished for the sins that they have chosen and have refused to give up. We must never sentimentalize people who have knowingly chosen the way of destruction (Rom. 1:32).

Ultimately, as Paul Helm observes, the eternal punishment of the wicked is a matter of "divine sovereignty": "All such questions, if pressed long and far enough, come down to the matter of the ultimate will and purpose of God."[4] God owes salvation to no one. The fact that heaven will be populated with redeemed sinners is a tribute to God's unfathomable mercy. We leave the sober reality that hell will be populated with impenitent sinners to the untraceable wisdom of our sovereign God. In either case, God is bringing glory to Himself. Heaven particularly magnifies the mercy of God; hell particularly brings glory to the justice of God.[5]

Annihilationism

A second unbiblical view of what happens after death is really a cluster of views that are often loosely grouped under a single name: *annihilationism*.[6] Strictly speaking, annihilationism says that God will render His verdict against the wicked but that they will thereafter cease to exist. This cessation of existence will take place either at a person's death or at the final judgment. Thus, not to be saved is to be consigned to nonexistence.

This view is an improvement over universalism in a couple of ways. First, it acknowledges the Bible's distinction between the righteous and the wicked, right up to the time that God renders His judgment on a person. Second, it distinguishes, within eternity, the state of the righteous and the state of the wicked. The righteous will enter life; the wicked will be deprived of life. That deprivation is the punishment of God.

Annihilationism, however, counters the Bible's testimony in at least three ways. First, the Bible teaches that existence after death is conscious. This is true for the righteous (see 2 Cor. 5:8; Phil. 1:23; Rev. 6:9–11), and it is also no less true for the wicked, as Jesus' parable of Lazarus and the rich man shows us (Luke 16:19–31). In that parable, Jesus describes a rich man as dying and going to a place of conscious torment ("I am in anguish in this flame," 16:24). That torment is the just penalty for his life in sin.[7]

Second, Jesus teaches that after the final judgment, the righteous enter "eternal life" and the cursed depart into "eternal punishment" (Matt. 25:46).

The two phrases "eternal life" and "eternal punishment" are parallel. This means that the wicked will be as alive and conscious as the righteous are alive and conscious. The torment of the wicked is not momentary or temporary. It is perpetual: The smoke of their torment goes up forever and ever, and they have no rest, day or night" (Rev. 14:11).

Third, Jesus teaches that there will be degrees of punishment, just as there will be degrees of reward.[8] If there are degrees of punishment—if some receive a "light beating" (Luke 12:48) and others receive a "severe beating" (v. 47)— then annihilation is impossible. Annihilation levels the punishment of the wicked—all are treated the same way. Jesus, however, teaches that the severity of a person's punishment is according to the measure of that person's sins.

Why, then, does the Bible sometimes speak of the state of the wicked as "the second death" (Rev. 20:14) or "eternal destruction" (2 Thess. 1:9) if the wicked are not annihilated at some point after death? The "second death" no more annihilates the wicked than the "first death" annihilated them. "Death" does not mean "nonexistence." Rather, the word "death" captures the idea of a state of justly deserved punishment for sin (see Rom. 6:23). Similarly, the punishment of "eternal destruction" takes two words from our everyday experience and combines them to impress on us how terrible this condition is. It is a destruction that never completely destroys and never ends. It is an expression that presses the limits of our understanding. That, however, is the point. Hell is a terrible, terrible place to be.

Second Probation

A third unbiblical view is *second probation*. The word *probation* carries the older sense of "testing" or "trial." This view says that people will get the opportunity after they die to repent and believe in Christ. The window of salvation does not shut at death, according to this view. There is mercy available beyond the grave.

This view is certainly an improvement on the previous two. People exit this life either as sinners or as saints. Christ is the only way to salvation, and one must repent and believe in Christ to be saved.

The doctrine of second probation, however, is counter to the teaching of Scripture that the window of mercy closes at one's death (for a particular person) and at the return of Christ (for persons still living). First, when a person dies, his opportunity for salvation comes to an end. Our eternal destiny is tied to our life on earth. Paul tells us that "we must all appear before the judgment seat of Christ, so that each one may receive what is due for what he has done in the body, whether good or evil" (2 Cor. 5:10), and John writes, "Blessed are the dead who die in the Lord from now on. . . . For their deeds follow them!" (Rev. 14:13). What we do in this life—not anything that we may do after death—explains where we will spend eternity. Thus, Hebrews reminds us that after death we will be ushered straight into judgment (Heb. 9:27). There is neither mention of nor opportunity given for salvation in the interim between death and judgment. When Jesus tells His hearers to "repent or perish," He has in mind the life spans of His hearers on earth (Luke 13:3, 5). The context makes it clear that death ends the opportunity for one to repent (see vv. 2, 4). Since God has not said that He will grant salvation after one's death, those who die unsaved have no right to expect salvation after death.

Second, when Christ returns, it will be to judge the world in righteousness, not to save unreconciled sinners. The goats brought before their Judge will not be given an opportunity to be saved. Rather, the Judge will pronounce and then execute His sentence (see Matt. 25:33, 41, 46). To be sure, Jesus will consummate His saving work in the lives of His people when He returns.[9] In that way, He will "save those who are eagerly waiting for him" (Heb. 9:28). But His return is not intended to bring salvation to those who are then strangers to God's mercy and who are the enemies of God.

Purgatory

A fourth unbiblical view of life after death is the doctrine of purgatory. This is a teaching of the Roman Catholic Church. It was settled and raised to confessional status at the councils of Florence (1431–49) and Trent (1545–63), but it reflects a much older teaching that circulated throughout the medieval church. Purgatory, it needs to be stressed, concerns not the wicked but the righteous. It is a state, furthermore, to which most believers are said to go before they are admitted into heaven. As the Catechism of the Catholic Church describes it, "All who die in God's grace and friendship, but still imperfectly purified, are indeed assured of their eternal salvation; but after death they undergo purification, so as to achieve the holiness necessary to enter the joy of heaven."[10] The Council of Trent declares that "the souls detained there are helped by the acts of intercession of the faithful, and especially by the acceptable Sacrifice of the Altar."[11] This is why, in the Roman Catholic Church, there are prayers for the dead and Masses offered for the dead. These are thought to assist the souls in purgatory, effectively shortening their time there. According to Rome, Christ remits the *eternal* penalty for sin (a gift available to us in the Mass), but *temporal* punishments for sin must be paid by the sinner.[12] Since most of us have not done the latter in this life, we will need to do this work in purgatory. Only when we have "achieve[d] the holiness necessary to enter the joy of heaven" may we depart purgatory and go to heaven.

Rome's doctrine of purgatory is inseparable from Rome's doctrine of justification. According to Rome, the righteousness of Christ is infused into us, or worked into us, gradually. Only when we become truly and properly "righteous" may we enter into heaven. Justification is therefore a process and, for most of us, will not be complete in this life. That is why we need purgatory—those extra years will allow us to finish what we started but did not finish in this life.

The Bible teaches, however, that the sinner is justified by faith alone, apart from works—that is, anything that we have done, are doing, or ever will do (Gal. 2:16). Through faith in Christ, Christ's righteousness is imputed to us—that is, it is counted or reckoned to us in the courtroom of God (2 Cor. 5:21). Faith, which is the free gift of God, is purely receptive in justification. It receives—and adds nothing to—the righteousness of Christ that is counted to us for justification. Justification is not a change that God makes within us. Justification is God's counting the sinner righteous only for the righteousness of His Son imputed to the sinner and received through faith alone. Christ's righteousness—His perfect obedience and full satisfaction for sin—gives us sole and complete title to eternal life (Rom. 5:17).

The justified sinner, then, is entitled to enter heaven from the moment he puts his trust in Christ as He is offered in the gospel. That title is not his faith but the righteousness of Christ credited to him. Christ has fully paid the penalty due to the sinner for his sin. Having made full satisfaction to God's justice, Christ forever wipes all our debts clean. There is therefore no need for purgatory—God's people, justified through faith alone, have all they need in Christ to enter heaven immediately upon their deaths. Furthermore, and most importantly, the Bible makes no mention of purgatory. As the Westminster Confession of Faith puts the matter, "Besides these two places [heaven and hell], for souls separated from their bodies, the Scripture acknowledgeth none" (32.1). And there is no biblical reason to pray for or otherwise intercede for those who have died (see 2 Sam. 12:21–23). In the case of believers who have died, Scripture says that "their deeds follow them" (Rev. 14:13). They have finished their course and now "rest from their labors" in the heavenly rest that God has appointed for them.

What Does Happen after Death?

Having dispelled common unbiblical misconceptions about death, we may now think about the Bible's testimony to what happens after death. We may look at this teaching along two lines, following the summary of that teaching in Westminster Larger Catechism 86. There is what happens to the elect, and there is what happens to the wicked.

The Elect

As the catechism helpfully explains the Bible's teaching, after death "[the] souls [of the elect] are then made perfect in holiness, and received into the highest heavens, where they behold the face of God in light and glory, waiting for the full redemption of their bodies, which even in death continue united to Christ, and rest in their graves as in their beds, till at the last day they be again united to their souls" (WLC 86). The catechism considers what happens to the elect at death in light of the two components of their humanity, their souls and their bodies.

First, the soul will be made perfectly holy, and all sin will be removed from it. Thus, Hebrews speaks of the believing dead as "the spirits of the righteous made perfect" (Heb. 12:23). It is not just that God removes sin. It is that He makes the soul fully righteous. The soul is then ushered immediately into heaven. That is to say, the soul goes into the presence of Christ (Phil. 1:23), who is currently in heaven (Acts 3:20b–21). This is, in Paul's words, to be "at home with the Lord" (2 Cor. 5:6, 8). There, in the "presence" of God, David reminds us, the soul experiences "fullness of joy" and "pleasures forevermore" (Ps. 16:11). Perfectly holy. Perfectly happy.

Second, what about the body? The body is committed to the grave, of course, with the promise and hope of full redemption at the resurrection. This work of bodily resurrection, Paul tells us, is promised to us in our adoption as sons (Rom. 8:23). Yet even in death, the body remains united to Christ. The believing dead are "the dead in Christ" (1 Thess. 4:16). That is to say, every part of the believer remains united to Christ even in death. Death does not—cannot—sever the bond between Christ and the Christian. That is why, the catechism continues, referencing the prophet Isaiah, the bodies of believers "rest in their graves as in their beds"—"for the righteous man is taken away from calamity; he enters into peace; they rest in their beds who walk in their uprightness" (Isa. 57:1–2).

The Wicked

By contrast, the catechism continues, "the souls of the wicked are at their death cast into hell, where they remain in torments and utter darkness, and their bodies kept in their graves, as in their prisons, till the resurrection and judgment of the great day" (WLC 86). Here also, the catechism summarizes the Bible's teaching about the future of the wicked in terms of their souls and their bodies.

The souls of the wicked are, immediately upon death, cast into hell as a place of torment and darkness. The rich man in Jesus' parable cries out to Abraham, "I am in anguish in this flame" (Luke 16:24). If the wicked angels are now "kept in eternal chains under gloomy darkness until the judgment of the great day" (Jude 6), the same must be said of the souls of the wicked after they die. They are bound up in "gloomy darkness" as they await the judgment day.

Their bodies, like the bodies of the elect, are also committed to the grave, but they have no hope of a glorious resurrection awaiting them (only a resurrection of "shame and everlasting contempt," Dan. 12:2). The grave is not a bed to them but a detention cell. If the souls of angels and of the wicked are bound in "eternal chains," then the bodies of the wicked must experience something comparable. They are imprisoned in the grave until the judgment day.

Conclusion

Scripture is clear—death is final. The way that we close our eyes in death is the way that we awaken in eternity. We are, by nature, sinners and rebels against God. If that does not change before death, this is how we will enter and spend eternity. The good news, of course, is that God offers sinners mercy in Jesus Christ. The call of the gospel is to "be reconciled to God" (2 Cor. 5:20). Reconciliation can happen because God has taken the initiative, sending His Son into the world to live and die for sinners (5:21). By the power of the Holy Spirit, the Father draws sinners to His Son to find eternal life. God is ordinarily pleased to do this work of salvation in connection with the preaching of the gospel (Rom. 10:14–17). Sinners are perishing. There is hope only in Jesus. The window of salvation will not be open forever. There is an urgency to the work of evangelism and missions. We should be investing our prayers, our finances, and our time to further this work. How are we using the gifts and resources that God has given us? Are we committing them to spreading the gospel throughout the world, so that God's mercy may be exalted in the saving of sinners? The concern that we have for the salvation of others should never come at the cost of neglecting our own salvation. Just as Paul took care lest he himself "should be disqualified" though he had preached the gospel, have we ourselves repented from sin and turned in faith to Christ in the gospel (1 Cor. 9:27)?

In addition, Scripture is equally clear—every believer has a sure hope in the gospel. We will be made perfectly holy and happy. We will dwell in the very presence of our Savior. Our bodies, still united to Christ, await the promised resurrection. What is most precious to us about our hope? It is not freedom from sorrow and sin or the reunion we will have with believing loved ones—as certain and wonderful as these things are. It is that we will be in unbroken communion with our God—Father, Son, and Holy Spirit. This hope transcends any earthly hope or goal that we may have. This helps us understand why the Bible so often describes the people of God as a *pilgrim* people. We are on our way to the Celestial City, just as Abraham was before us (Heb. 11:8–10, 13–16). Do our lives reflect the fact that we are pilgrims? That we really don't have our home here? Are we preparing ourselves to dwell eternally with our great God? We don't prepare ourselves in order to earn our way into heaven. We prepare ourselves in light of the fact that Christ has already made the way for us into heaven and is now preparing a place for us (John 14:1–3). And the more we set our minds on heaven, the more we will want to serve Christ on earth. Let's use our gifts and graces to glorify on earth the God in whose presence we will dwell forever in heaven!

4

Why Did
Christ Die?

S o far, we have been thinking about death in the experience of fallen human beings. Death ushers people immediately into the presence of their Maker and Judge. Any and all who have put their trust in Christ on this earth step into the presence of the One who is also their Redeemer. Death, then, is the portal to life. Leaving this life, we enter the fullness of eternal life. Death, as the wages of sin, is fearful. Believers are not immune from experiencing fears connected with death. What allows us to silence those fears is the hope in Christ that is ours in the gospel.

In this chapter, we are going to probe that hope. What did Christ do that we should be delivered from death and brought into everlasting life? The biblical answer, of course, is that He died and was raised from the dead.

On the face of it, it is strange that Jesus should die. Jesus was (and is) altogether righteous. When He was conceived in the womb of the Virgin Mary, He was "holy" (Luke 1:35). When He hung on the cross in dying agony, the centurion pronounced Him "righteous" (Luke 23:47, author's translation). Jesus could say to His enemies what you and I could never say to anyone: "Which one of you convicts me of sin?" (John 8:46). Hebrews declares the exalted Jesus "holy, innocent, unstained, separated from sinners, and exalted above the heavens" (Heb. 7:26). From conception to exaltation, Jesus is altogether righteous.

Here, then, is the problem. If Christ never ceased to be righteous, if He "knew no sin" (2 Cor. 5:21), then why did He die? Death, after all, is the penalty for sin. Jesus was not a sinner by nature, and He never committed a single sin in His life. He alone of all human beings who have ever walked the earth didn't deserve to die. Yet He did die. Why?

The answer to that question will help us better understand our hope in the gospel. We will better grasp what the Savior has done to deliver us from death and to win for us life. We will better be able to meet the fears that death can often send into our lives.

To explore this hope, we will first think about the Bible's teaching on union with Christ. We will then explore what Christ's life, death, and resurrection mean for us who are united with Him. We will finally think about how Christ's life, death, and resurrection transform death for His people.

Union with Christ

Central to the Bible's teaching about salvation is union with Christ. We may look at the biblical doctrine of union with Christ along four lines.

First, Christ, the second person of the Godhead, united Himself to our humanity. He did this when He assumed into union with His deity a true, real human nature.[1] Jesus did not have a body or a human soul in eternity to bring with Him to earth. He assumed humanity in the womb of the Virgin Mary. His humanity was "conceived by the power of the Holy Ghost, . . . of [Mary's] substance" (WCF 8.2). He was "born of woman, born under the law" (Gal. 4:4). His humanity was conceived when "the power of the Most High . . . overshadow[ed] [Mary]" (Luke 1:35).

How may we describe the humanity of Jesus Christ? His body was just like ours; His soul was just like ours.[2] This is the testimony of the Gospels. Jesus experienced hunger, thirst, weariness, and sleep. Jesus was angry, joyful, and compassionate. The only difference between Jesus' humanity and ours is that His was entirely sinless. This is why Paul states that Jesus was "born in the likeness of men" and that the Father sent "his own Son in the likeness of sinful flesh" (Phil. 2:7; Rom. 8:3). Paul is not saying that Jesus was "humanlike." Jesus became a true, real, complete man. What Paul is saying is that He was a human being in every way that we are, except for sin.

Why did Jesus become a human being? The biblical answer is that to fulfill God's eternal purpose to redeem human beings, the Son of God had to become a human being to save them. The author to the Hebrews tells us: "For surely it is not angels that he helps, but he helps the offspring of Abraham. Therefore he had to be made like his brothers in every respect, so that he might become a merciful and faithful high priest in the service of God, to make propitiation for the sins of the people" (Heb. 2:16–17). Jesus "helps" humans, not angels. The kind of help that He offers is the help of a "high priest in the service of God," one who "make[s] propitiation for the sins of the people." For Him to offer that kind of help, Hebrews tells us, He "had to be made like his brothers in every respect." It would not have helped us for Him to become an angel, or to become something resembling a human being, or to become a partial human being. He had to become a true, complete human being. No other could save us.

Second, we, in turn, must be united to Christ in time, if we are to share in Christ and benefit from what He has done for us.[3] As Paul tells us in 1 Corinthians 15:22, "For as in Adam all die, so also in Christ shall all be made alive." The only way that we can experience eternal life is to be brought into union with Christ. There is no such life outside Christ. Once we are in Christ, death has passed, and life has come. John puts it starkly: "Whoever has the Son has life; whoever does not have the Son of God does not have life" (1 John 5:12); or, as Paul reminded the Corinthians, "If anyone is in Christ, new creation" (2 Cor. 5:17, author's translation).[4]

Third, how should we think of the union between Christ and the believer? By nature we are separated from God and not "joined to the Lord" (1 Cor. 6:17), but this is exactly what happens at the very outset of our Christian experience. How is this bond forged? We may think of this along two lines.

In the first place, the Holy Spirit is the bond of our union with Christ. He unites us to Christ. The Holy Spirit unites the sinner to Christ such that Christ dwells in us by His Spirit. All those who are "in Christ," Paul reasons, are also "in the Spirit" (Rom. 8:1–2, 9). To be "in the Spirit" means that "the Spirit of God dwells in you. Anyone who does not have the Spirit of Christ does not belong to him" (v. 9). For "the Spirit of God [to dwell] in you" is to say that "Christ is in you" (v. 10). Every believer is "in Christ" and Christ is in every believer. Every believer is "in the Spirit" and the Spirit is in every believer. Christ and the Spirit always work in tandem.[5] The Holy Spirit is the bond of our union with Jesus Christ.

In the second place, the Spirit unites us to Christ *through faith*. Paul tells the Ephesians that "Christ ... dwell[s] in your hearts through faith" (Eph.

3:17). Since Christ "lives in me," Paul tells the Galatians, "the life I now live in the flesh I live by faith in the Son of God" (Gal. 2:20). Faith, which is the gift of God (Eph. 2:8; Phil. 1:29), is the channel of one's bond with Christ. The life, then, of a person who is united to Christ is the life of faith. That *the Spirit* unites us to Christ underscores the "absolute sovereignty and sheer grace of God in our salvation." That we are united to Christ *by faith* helps us to see that "in belonging to Christ there is a 'mutuality' or 'covenant bond.'"[6]

Fourth, in light of the fact that Christ united Himself to our humanity and that we have been united to Christ by the Spirit through faith, what belongs to us in union with Him? The short answer is "everything!" We have every blessing that God ever gives His people in Jesus Christ. "Blessed be the God and Father of our Lord Jesus Christ, who has blessed us in Christ with every spiritual blessing in the heavenly places" (Eph. 1:3). Yet we have something higher still. What could be higher or greater than "every spiritual blessing in the heavenly places"? It is Christ Himself. Later, in Ephesians 5:25–27, Paul asserts that the church is to Christ as a bride is to her bridegroom. We, the church, are espoused to Christ. As a bridegroom gives himself to his bride, Christ has given Himself to His church. He is ours and, of course, we are His (1 Cor. 6:19–20).

Christ for Us—His Life, Death, and Resurrection

Now that we have seen that the whole of our salvation is ours in union with Christ, and that we belong to Him and He belongs to us in a most intimate relationship, we can ask an additional set of questions. What is it that Christ has done for us to bring blessing to us? If "every spiritual blessing" is ours in Christ, how has Christ's work secured such blessing for us? We may begin to answer these questions by thinking about the life, death, and resurrection of Christ.

There is, first, the life of Christ. What marked His life more than anything else was His obedience to His Father. Jesus told His disciples early in His ministry, "My food is to do the will of him who sent me and to accomplish his work" (John 4:34). Near the end of His earthly life, Jesus prayed to the Father, "I glorified you on earth, having accomplished the work that you gave me to do" (17:4). Paul emphasizes Jesus' life of obedience, culminating in His crowning act of obedience, His death on the cross (Phil. 2:8). This obedience,

Paul tells us elsewhere, is for the benefit of believers: "So by the one man's obedience the many will be made righteous" (Rom. 5:19b). It is imputed to us and received by faith alone for justification. Christ's obedience here stands in stark contrast with Adam's disobedience (which, in Adam, is *our* disobedience) (v. 19a). We need the last Adam to obey where the first Adam—and we in Adam—disobeyed. Christ obeyed in our place, and His obedience becomes ours through faith.

Second, there is the death of Christ. Christ died on the cross and accomplished something there. The Bible speaks with one voice. The Old Testament, from the perspective of anticipation, and the New Testament, from the perspective of fulfillment, speak of Christ's death as a sacrifice for sin (Isa. 52:13–53:12; Rom. 3:21–26; Heb. 9:11–28; 1 Peter 2:24). As sinners, we are guilty before God—that is, liable to His just penalty for sin. Jesus died as a sacrifice to take away sinners' guilt. His death redeems us from the guilt of sin (Rom. 3:24) and provides the sole foundation for our pardon by God (4:7–8). As sinners, we are also justly subject to the wrath of God. Jesus' sacrificial death is propitiatory. God sent Jesus into the world not only to make sacrifice for sins but, in making that sacrifice, to appease God's wrath against sinners (3:25; compare 1:18; 1 John 2:2). Through faith in Christ, we are reconciled to God and no longer subject to His wrath (Rom. 5:9–10).

Christ did not die for any sins of His own (He had none). Our sins were laid on Him, imputed to Him (Isa. 53:6). God therefore justly dealt with His Son on the cross as a sinner: "[God] made him to be sin who knew no sin" (2 Cor. 5:21). In union with Christ, we experienced the transfer of our sins to Christ. In His death, Christ made full satisfaction to God for our sins.

Third, there is the resurrection of Christ. Christ rose from the dead. Like the death of Christ, the resurrection sits at the very heart and center of the gospel (see 1 Cor. 15:1–3). Christ rose from the dead not merely to fulfill prophecy or merely to prove His deity. His resurrection was for us and for our salvation. That is why Paul tells the Corinthians that "if Christ has not been raised, your faith is futile and you are still in your sins" (1 Cor. 15:17). He was "raised for our justification" (Rom. 4:25; compare 1 Tim. 3:16). What is the connection between His resurrection and our salvation, particularly our justification? When Christ died, He died as One accursed of God for the sins of His people. The resurrection was the Father's lifting the sentence of condemnation from His Son. Jesus, our substitute, therefore passed judicially from condemnation to vindication. When He emerged from the grave, death was a defeated enemy. That is why Paul tells us that Christ has "abolished death" (2 Tim. 1:10). But Christ in His resurrection not only conquered death but also secured eternal life. And so He has "brought life and immortality to light through the gospel" (v. 10). This resurrection life He shares with us by the Holy Spirit (1 Cor. 15:45; 2 Cor. 3:17).

Christ's Life, Death, and Resurrection . . . and Death

Taken as a whole, Christ's saving work for us—His life, death, and resurrection—completely transforms death for us. In the first place, Christ's obedience has won life for us. Paul twice quotes this statement from the law: "If a person does them, he shall live by them" (Lev. 18:5; see Rom. 10:5; Gal. 3:12). That statement is a good summary of the principle that informs the covenant that God made with Adam in the garden.[7] Had Adam obeyed God, he would have entered into confirmed and heightened fellowship and communion with God. But Adam disobeyed, and the result was death, not only for himself but for all who are "in Adam." The last Adam, however, obeyed God. As a result, He secured life, not only for Himself but for all who are "in Christ." This is the point that Paul makes in Romans 5:17: "Those who receive the abundance of grace and the free gift of righteousness [will] reign in life through the one man Jesus Christ." And in 5:18: "So one act of righteousness leads to justification and life for all men." Jesus obeyed *for us*, and the result was life *for us*. *Jesus* obeyed, and *we* live! Every believer in Christ possesses a title to eternal life. Nothing, not even death, can take that life away from him (Col. 3:4).

In the next place, Christ died in our place to pay the penalty for sin that we owe. That atoning, propitiatory death was His victory over the devil and His liberation of His people from bondage to the fear of death. And so, in light of Christ's propitiation on the cross (Heb. 2:17), the writer to the Hebrews can say that Christ "through death" has "destroy[ed] the one who has the power of death, that is, the devil," and has rescued us from the enslavement of the "fear of death" (2:14–15). The cross, Paul writes, is the Father's "triumph," through Christ, over the demonic "rulers and authorities" (Col. 2:15), even as the cross means the "canceling [of] the record of debt that stood against us with its legal demands" (v. 14), and the "forgive[ness of] all our trespasses"

(v. 13). The sacrificial death of Christ has nullified death as the penalty for sin for the believer. It has thereby robbed the devil of the basis of his claim in our lives—namely, our sin and its unanswered guilt before God. Jesus has done this by paying the penalty for sin, by being condemned for us, by bearing the Father's wrath for us—all on the cross. Now that we are in Christ and share in His death, we stand in an entirely new relationship to death. Why do believers no longer fear death? It is because it cannot do us harm.

Finally, Christ rose again from the dead so that we might pass from condemnation to justification (Rom. 4:25). We are united to the resurrected, vindicated Christ. In raising Jesus from the dead, the Father vindicated His righteous Son. In light of the finished work of Christ at the cross, the Father lifted the sentence of condemnation from His Son. Death no longer had any claim on Christ. Neither, then, are His people subject to death. Therefore, the Father also vindicates us who are united to Him and to whom the righteousness of Christ has been credited and received through faith. When Paul asks, "Who is to condemn?" (Rom. 8:34), he appeals not only to the death of Christ but also to His resurrection: "Christ Jesus is the one who died—more than that, who was raised" (v. 34). The resurrection declares the reality that "there is . . . now no condemnation for those who are in Christ Jesus" (v. 1). We are no longer under the sentence of death as the penalty for sin.

Christ's resurrection was also His entrance, by the power of the Spirit, to the life of the age to come. His resurrected humanity is imperishable, glorious, powerful, and spiritual (see 1 Cor. 15:42–44). United to the risen Christ, we have already begun to experience resurrection life through the ministry of the Spirit (see Eph. 2:4–10). This life is currently inward and unseen. Our bodies remain "mortal," "dead because of sin" (Rom. 8:11, 10). We will fully experience resurrection life only when our bodies are raised from the dead, conformed to Christ's resurrection body (Phil. 3:21). Christ's resurrection leaves us in no doubt—we will experience resurrection life to the full, and death cannot bar us from possessing that life!

At the end of his great "resurrection chapter" (1 Cor. 15), Paul puts a boast in the believer's mouth. In context, it relates to the resurrection of Christ (and our resurrection in Him). But it no less applies to the glorious reality that Jesus' obedience, death, *and* resurrection are unchangeably and irreversibly ours: "The sting of death is sin, and the power of sin is the law. But thanks be to God, who gives us the victory through our Lord Jesus Christ" (1 Cor. 15:56–57). By His obedience, death, and resurrection, Christ has won complete, irreversible *victory* over death. That victory is ours, and it is ours in union with the risen Son of God.

Conclusion

The only hope to be had in the face of death is found in the Lord Jesus Christ. He is the God-man, God in the flesh, who assumed our humanity in order to live, die, and rise again for us and our salvation. We are disqualified from saving anyone else, much less ourselves. We are by nature sinners, justly subject to death in all its forms. Christ, however, was, is, and ever will be righteous. This righteous man, by His obedience, death, and resurrection, came in from the outside and destroyed death from the inside. That destruction is complete and irreversible.

The most important question that we can ask ourselves is "Am I in Christ?" The only way that we can benefit from His work for sinners, sharing in His great victory, is by belonging to Him. How do we know if we belong to Christ? Have we put *faith* in Him? Can we say with Paul that "we walk by faith, not by sight" (2 Cor. 5:7)? That "the life I now live in the flesh I live by faith in the Son of God, who loved me and gave himself for me" (Gal. 2:20)? Is there evidence that the *Spirit* has taken up residence in my life? Do I have the mindset of the Spirit (Rom. 8:5)? Do I pursue the lifestyle that is pleasing to the Spirit (v. 4)? Is my whole life being directed by the Spirit (Gal. 5:18), and am I trying to "keep in step with the Spirit" (5:25)?

This is not to say that we are sinless—no Christian is in this life (see 1 John 1:8–10). Nor is it to say that our faith or the fruit of the Spirit can deliver us from death or make us right with God—it cannot. Only Christ can deliver us and bring us to salvation and life. Rather, faith and the evidencing work of the Spirit are streams that lead us to their source, the One who has won the victory, Jesus Christ. We must put our trust in Him alone and always.

Further, God does not want us to be content with a general or vague grasp of the obedience, death, and resurrection of Christ for salvation. Scripture goes to great pains to explain *how* the work of Christ has brought an end to death and has won entrance into everlasting life. We, then, should take pains to study Scripture, pause over these great truths, meditate on them, and internalize them.

One reason that we should do this is that each of us must prepare to experience death one day. When that day comes, Satan will be ready to tempt us to despair. The world will offer us no spiritual comfort or aid. Our remaining unbelief will do its best to cast darkness over our souls. *That* is when we need the armament that the gospel alone supplies. Tellingly, the first piece of armor that Paul details when he describes "the whole armor of God" (Eph. 6:13) is "the belt of truth" (6:14). And the last-named piece of armor is "the sword of the Spirit, which is the word of God" (6:17). We need minds that are renewed and transformed by grace (see Rom. 12:2; Eph. 4:23), minds that are thoroughly equipped with Bible truth. When we find ourselves in "the valley of the shadow of death," when death's shadow tries to cast itself over our dying selves, we may say with David, grasping the truth of Scripture, "I will fear no evil, for you are with me; your rod and your staff, they comfort me" (Ps. 23:4). We can say these things in full confidence because, in Christ, "all things are [ours]," whether "life or death" (1 Cor. 3:21–22). Are you preparing for that day?

5

Why Do
Christians Die?

O ne of the paradoxes of the gospel is that Jesus Christ, who is "life"
(1 John 1:2), died on a Roman cross. He died, of course, to conquer
death and to win life for His people. We see at Calvary what John Owen
famously termed "the death of death in the death of Christ."

That raises a question. If Christ dealt death the deathblow, and if He has
delivered His people from death, then why do those who are "in Christ" die?
Wouldn't it stand to reason that Christians should escape death altogether?

This is a question that the Westminster Larger Catechism takes up
directly. One of the blessings of church history is that believers who have
gone before us have thought long and hard about the difficult questions of
the Christian life. Their reflections and writings are not, of course, infallible.
They must be tested against the standard of God's infallible Word, the Bible.
And for nearly four centuries, believers have found the Westminster Standards (of which the Larger Catechism is part) to be a tremendous aid to the
study of Scripture's teaching.

In that spirit, we will come to the Larger Catechism to help find a biblical answer to the question, Why is it that believers die? We will look at the
way that it asks the question, the answer that it gives, and the biblical support
for that answer. To close this chapter, we will think through some fears that
believers may face as we approach death.

The Death of Christians

Why is it that Christians die? Here is how the Larger Catechism asks the question:

> Death being the wages of sin, why are not the righteous delivered from death, seeing all their sins are forgiven in Christ? (WLC 85)

In this question, the catechism posits two matters that are critical to thinking about death in a biblical way. The first is that death is the "wages of sin." This statement, of course, is a reference to Romans 6:23 ("the wages of sin is death").[1] In the world of employment, a wage is something that you are owed for work that you have done. In a similar way, when we sin, we earn, and are therefore owed, death. The second is that all the sins of believers are forgiven in Christ. Every believer, we have seen, is justified in Christ. That is, sinners who put their faith in Christ as He is offered in the gospel are counted righteous in Christ. The basis of that declaration ("righteous") is not anything in ourselves, not even our faith. It is entirely the righteousness of Christ, imputed or credited to us, and received through faith alone. This righteousness, the Bible teaches, is the perfect obedience of Christ and His full satisfaction for sin. The moment that God justifies the sinner, the penalty is lifted. His debts are paid. He is no longer under condemnation. Justice has been satisfied. The wrath of God has been propitiated.

The problem, as the catechism observes, comes when we put these two biblical truths together. If death is the penalty of sin, and if Christ has fully paid that penalty, and if, in Christ, we are justified, shouldn't we be altogether delivered from death? How could we possibly die?

We could put the matter more sharply. Doesn't this dilemma raise questions about the justice of God? We don't allow double jeopardy in our judicial system—justice forbids condemning and punishing a person after that person has already been legally acquitted of his crime. If we have been justified, not merely pardoned but counted righteous, isn't it unjust for us to suffer death, the wages of sin? Is there double jeopardy in the courtroom of God? Does the gospel contain some fine print or an escape clause that we have missed? Has God attached some legal disclaimer to His pledge to forgive all our sins in Christ, such that we fall back under condemnation?

The answer to all these questions is a resounding "No!" In saying that, we should recognize up front that the Bible gives us "some truths which shed some light on the problem. But the problem itself cannot be wholly solved."[2] This is just one difficulty we encounter in Scripture that does not admit of a complete solution. God may not give us enough to satisfy every question we may have here, but He gives us enough to know that He works "for his own glory and the real good of his people."[3] We have enough to emerge from this question confident in the justice and goodness of God, the sufficiency of the work of Christ for sinners, and the truth of the gospel. Armed with this confidence, we must face death as we face life: "by faith, not by sight" (2 Cor. 5:7).

The Larger Catechism then offers a biblical answer to the question it has posed:

> The righteous shall be delivered from death itself at the last day, and even in death are delivered from the sting and curse of it; so that, although they die, yet it is out of God's love, to free them perfectly from sin and misery, and to make them capable of further communion with Christ in glory, which they then enter upon. (WLC 85)

For believers, God, in Christ, has transformed death in a twofold way. He has taken something away from death, and He has added something to death. We may look at each now.

What God, in Christ, Has Taken from Death

In Christ, the catechism reminds us, we "shall be delivered from death itself at the last day." Believers "are not delivered from death as an *experience*," but "the righteous are delivered from the death of the body as a *state* or *condition*."[4] In other words, although Christians die, it is not because death is their unchecked master. Christ came to "deliver all those who through fear of death were subject to lifelong slavery" (Heb. 2:15). Although believers die, they die in the expectation of complete deliverance from death at the resurrection.

Further, "even in death [we] are delivered from the sting and curse of it." Behind this statement is what Paul tells the Corinthians: "'O death, where is your victory? O death, where is your sting?' The sting of death is sin, and the power of sin is the law. But thanks be to God, who gives us the victory through our Lord Jesus Christ" (1 Cor. 15:55–57, quoting Hos. 13:14). In Christ, death has lost its sting. Death's sting is sin, and sin's power is the law. Since Christ has satisfied our obligations to the law—paying its penalty and meeting its demands—death has no sting for the believer. Believers, Paul asserts, do not experience death as the judicial sentence of God. It is not the punishment of an unreconciled Judge. This transformed experience of death is entirely owing to what Christ has accomplished for us in His obedience, death, and resurrection.

What God, in Christ, Has Added to Death

Jesus Christ has delivered His people from the state of death as curse. And even in the experience of death, death for them is in no way penal. But God, in Christ, has done more than take away. He has also added something to death, something that transforms death.

The catechism points us to God's disposition toward us when we die: "Although they die, yet it is out of God's love." The phrase "although they die" captures the Bible's teaching that death is the last enemy. It is not a positive good. Yet even though believers die, their death proceeds not from God's vindicatory justice but from His fatherly love. God, in love, sent His only begotten Son into this world to save sinners (John 3:16). God, in love, did not spare His own Son but gave Him up for us all (Rom. 8:32). Death may not itself be a positive good, but it is something that God appoints *for* our good (see v. 28). God sovereignly appoints the death of each individual, and He does so, in love, for each and every one of His people.

This is why Paul can tell the Philippians that, on balance, he prefers death to life. He tells them that his "desire is to depart and be with Christ, for that is far better" (Phil. 1:23). In that sense, Paul can look forward to death—not for the experience or event of death itself, but for what death, in God's providence, will bring to him. While death may not be good, it is nevertheless for the good of the one who trusts in Christ.

What, then, is the good that death, in God's hands, works for the believer? The catechism describes that good, biblically, along two lines. First, God intends, through death, to "free [us] perfectly from sin and misery." When a person comes to faith in Christ, he is instantly delivered from the guilt and condemnation of sin (Rom. 8:1). He is also immediately delivered from the dominion of sin (6:6–7, 11, 14). But sin continues to indwell the believer (7:17) and grieve the believer (7:24). We are perfectly freed from sin and misery only at the moment of death. At death, we join the "spirits of the righteous made perfect" (Heb. 12:23). Our souls—our minds, our wills, and our affections—are completely freed from the presence and influence of sin. Sin will no longer affect our relationships with other people and with God. More than that, as Johannes Vos reminds us, we are brought from "this environment of sin and misery to the perfect environment of heavenly peace and rest."[5] Not only is sin removed from us, but we are removed from sin and all its effects and influences on our souls.

Second, in death, we are made "capable of further communion with Christ in glory, which [we] then enter upon." As we have seen, when the believer dies, he goes to what Scripture calls Abraham's bosom (Luke 16:22), paradise (23:43), and the presence of Christ (Phil. 1:23). As believers, we have communed with Christ in grace. United to Him by the Spirit and through faith, we are justified in Christ, are adopted in Christ, and are being sanctified in Christ. We have had foretastes and glimpses of glory in Christ (2 Cor. 3:18; 1 Peter 1:8). At death, our communion with Christ does not come to an end. On the contrary, we immediately enter a newer and richer experience of communion with Christ. We commune with the same Christ, but we commune with Him *in glory*. It is for this reason that Paul pronounces the departed believer's presence with Christ to be "far better" (Phil. 1:23).

What makes communion with Christ in glory preferable to communion with Christ in grace? For one thing, "the sins and temptations of [our] own heart[s] and the distractions of earthly life will have passed away." All that entices us away from fellowship with Christ will be removed. Furthermore, "bodily weakness, weariness, infirmity, sickness, and pain will be no more." The bodily pains and infirmities that can diminish the richness of our experience of communion with Christ will be a thing of the past. And best of all, we will be in "the visible presence of Christ in glory."[6] Our souls will see the One we love, not in the shame and weakness that marked His presence on earth, but in the glory and power that mark His presence in heaven. We will see Him and we will be near Him!

For all these reasons, we say with the psalmist, "Precious in the sight of the LORD is the death of his saints" (Ps. 116:15). We say "Amen" to the heavenly voice and to the Spirit's words recorded by the Apostle John: "'Blessed are the dead who die in the Lord from now on.' 'Blessed indeed,' says the Spirit" (Rev. 14:13). Only our God could take something as awful and miserable as death and make it the instrument of working unimaginably good things in the lives of His children!

Facing Fears in Death

A recent hymn teaches us to sing, "No guilt in life, / no fear in death: / this is the pow'r of Christ in me."[7] This verse expresses biblical truth. Believers have no guilt in the courtroom of God—we have been justified by faith in Christ. And believers have no cause to fear death. Christ has conquered death and has removed for us death's sting and curse.

And yet the specter of death presents fears and temptations to every believer. Death is not a positive good. It is an evil, an intruder, an enemy. Satan, the world, and the flesh will exploit this reality in an attempt to draw believers away from God. This is never so true as in the hour of death.

If we find ourselves scared of death or afraid in the approach of death, this does not mean that we are not Christians, but being a Christian means that we are not enslaved to these fears. We have resources in the gospel that help us to face those fears in faith and courage. We have a Christian duty when these fears become real to us.

Older writers spoke directly and at length to this very issue. They knew that Christians face these fears and that they were not simply going to disappear on their own. They also knew that Christians had been freed from being mastered by these fears. They wanted to help God's people meet these fears in faith.

At the dawn of the Reformation, Martin Luther preached a sermon, "A Sermon on Preparing to Die," that equips believers to face the fears that so often accompany death.[8] The early English Puritan William Perkins published a treatise in 1597, *A Salve for a Sick Man*. In this treatise, addressing sickness and death, Perkins wants to help believers to "d[ie] well" and, to that end, urges his audience how "not to fear death overmuch."[9] In the next century, the English Puritan Edward Pearse, who died of tuberculosis at age forty, authored a brief work designed to help Christians prepare themselves for death. "A dying hour," he writes early in that book, "is a difficult hour," and Christians need to be ready to face the challenges that accompany death's approach.[10] In his well-known treatise *Man's Fourfold State*, the eighteenth-century Scottish pastor Thomas Boston devotes several pages to guiding readers in "how to prepare for death, so that we may die comfortably."[11]

As pastors, part of the way that these men shepherded their flocks was to offer biblical guidance, in pulpit and in pen, about facing the fears and terrors that can accompany the death even of Christian people. What, then, are some of the fears that we may face? How do we meet them with the truth of the gospel? How may we prepare ourselves so that we may "have [an] abundant entrance ministered to us into heaven and glory"?[12]

We may take up three fears in particular that may confront and trouble Christians. The first is the *fear of readiness*: "What if I'm not ready to meet Christ in the hour of death? My sins are many. I'm not as holy as I should be. Death is final. What if I leave this earth unprepared?" Certainly, we may sympathize with this concern. It is no small thing to appear before our Maker and the Judge of all people. A conscience that is not deadened is keenly aware of one's sins of omission and commission. Satan, who is an "accuser of [the] brothers" (Rev. 12:10), strives to sow despair in the souls of the dying. He will not only call to mind the sins of believers but also try to persuade us that we have never truly repented and believed in Christ, that God would never accept us, and that we have sinned away the day of mercy.

The only firm foundation that we have at this—or any other—moment is the gospel of God. The gospel tells us that we are delivered from death and brought into life not by our own doing but by the doing of another, Jesus Christ. Our sins are freely pardoned by the blood of Christ and not at all by the works of our own hands. We are accepted in Christ on the basis of His perfect obedience and full satisfaction alone. And that righteousness is credited to us and received through faith alone. That faith does not even make us acceptable to God. Scripture declares that God "justifies the ungodly" (Rom. 4:5). Christ "died for the ungodly" (5:6), and the Father set His love upon us entirely by grace and not at all by our works (11:5–6; 9:14–15). In brief, "Salvation belongs to the LORD!" (Jonah 2:9).

This gospel is the gospel *of God*. It is His truth and not ours. We say, with the Apostle, "Let God be true though every one were a liar" (Rom. 3:4). Christ, who is the way, the truth, and the life, has freely and sincerely invited us to Himself in the gospel of grace. All who come to Him in faith He will never cast out (John 6:37). Our hope is grounded entirely on the mercy of God in Christ. Whether we have been trusting Him for our whole lives or for just a few moments, it is *Christ* who saves the sinner. When conscience convicts or Satan accuses, we must go straight to Christ, find in Him our refuge, and hide under His wings. We will never find safety or peace in ourselves. We will always find safety and peace in Jesus Christ. We may meet death in confidence and victory only if our hopes are firmly and entirely grounded in His merits on our behalf.

A second fear that we may face is the *fear of loss*. Death, we have seen, is loss. We are losing our families, our church families, our friends. We are leaving work unfinished, opportunities untouched, and goals unrealized. Adding to the grief of that loss is the uncertainty surrounding it all: "Who will care for my loved ones? Will anyone ever finish what I started to do but will never complete?"

When such fears meet us, we should remember that the timing and circumstances of our death are not accidental. God has set all those details by His eternal, unchangeable decree. The decree that appointed each of us to dwell in a particular family, to be part of a particular church, and to have a particular set of friends is the same decree that has appointed us to part from them at a specific time. The decree that ordained that we would have gifts and graces to serve others in our homes, our churches, and our places of work is the same decree that has ordered us to lay down the exercise of those gifts and graces in this world at a particular moment. Remember that the One who has decreed these things is the Father of the believer. He has not done these things in spite or as an act of vengeance. Far from it. Even the hard and difficult circumstances surrounding our death proceed from the care, love, and wisdom of our Father in heaven. He will never give what is for our destruction but will give only what is for our good. We must trust that His way is both wise and good. We must trust that His way is what is best—for His glory and for our eternal good.

We must also remember that God is the God of the widow and the orphan (see Deut. 10:18; Pss. 68:5; 146:9). Widows and orphans were two of the most vulnerable kinds of people in ancient societies, and they often still are. They lacked networks of family to provide for and to protect them. God therefore engages Himself to provide for and to protect the most vulnerable among His people. We see that care for widows extending into the New Testament (see Acts 6:1–7; 9:36–43; 1 Tim. 5:1–16)—God has not changed. As we prepare to depart this world in death, there is none better to whom we may commit our spouses, our children, and all our other loved ones than this God.

How, then, do we meet this fear of loss? We remember that in the gospel, God is our heavenly Father. He cares for us and provides for us in wisdom. He wants and accomplishes what is for our eternal good. He pledges Himself to watch over our loved ones when we are no longer able to be with them in this life. We can trust God to keep His word and to honor His promises.

A third fear that we may face is the *fear of pain*. Death can be painful. Painful in soul, painful in body: "What if the days and hours leading up to my death are painful? What if those pains are more than I can bear? What if I give way? If my death is painful and a dark time for me spiritually, will that mean that I'm not a Christian?"

The first thing to keep in mind is that God nowhere promises to spare believers in this life the various trials of soul and of body that people experience in this world. As Solomon reminds us: "It is the same for all, since the same event happens to the righteous and the wicked, to the good and the evil, to the clean and the unclean, to him who sacrifices and him who does not sacrifice. As the good one is, so is the sinner" (Eccl. 9:2). That is why you cannot distinguish a Christian and a non-Christian based on what happens to each in the providence of God. Some unbelievers have left this world in apparent serenity. Some Christians have suffered in body and soul as they approach death. A death that is free of pain does not mean that one is a Christian, and a death that is painful and difficult does not mean that one is not a Christian.

William Perkins records some of John Calvin's last words: "I mourned as a dove. . . . Lord, You grind me to powder, but it suffices me because it is Your hand."[13] Notice what Calvin does here. He testifies to his pain and distress and confesses that these have come to him from the hand of God. He gladly submits himself to his Father's will and power. He cries out to his God in his distress. Calvin's response is the response of faith. Calvin shows us how Christians may face even painful deaths.

A second thing to remember is that Jesus Christ, who was and is beloved by the Father, was not spared pains of body or of soul in death. The amazing thing is that He did not have to do this! He chose to do it out of love for us, in order to save us from sin and death. Christ is our forerunner. He has gone before us and has sanctified death and the grave to us. Every believer is united to Christ, even and especially in the moments approaching death. Whatever the circumstances surrounding our death, and whether our death is painful or pain-free, we know that Jesus is present with us by His Spirit. We are never alone. He will not leave or forsake us at our greatest trial. He is interceding for us. He is helping us and comforting us by the ministry of the Spirit. In life and in death, "the eternal God is your dwelling place, and underneath are the everlasting arms" (Deut. 33:27).

Equipping Ourselves in Life

The time to prepare ourselves to meet these fears is not the days and hours before our death. It is right now. Scripture calls us to prepare ourselves for death while we live. We may think of three ways to do this. Each has to do with our minds (Rom. 12:2).

First, we must think more, not less, about death. We live in a world that denies death and does its best to distract itself from its inevitability. The gospel teaches us to look at death not only for what it is but also in light of how Christ has transformed it for His people. The more we discipline ourselves to think biblically about death now, the better prepared we will be to face any fears that may come alongside death when it eventually arrives. Luther told his congregation: "We should familiarize ourselves with death during our lifetime, inviting death into our presence when it is still at a distance and not on the move. . . . You must look at death while you are alive and see sin in the light of grace, and hell in the light of heaven, permitting nothing to divert you from that view."[14] Thomas Boston reminds us that "the less you think on death, the thoughts of it will be the more frightful: make it familiar to you by frequent meditations upon it, and you may thereby quiet your fears. . . . [Saints] ought to be always on good terms with death."[15]

Second, as we think of death, think of what we will exchange—this life, a vale of tears, for the life to come, where there is no weeping or sighing; this life, marked by sin and misery, for the life to come, marked by glory and blessedness. To be sure, "to live is Christ," but "to die is gain" (Phil. 1:21). For this reason, the Puritans preached on the text "the day of death [is better] than the day of birth" (Eccl. 7:1).[16] The sermon that the Puritan Thomas Brooks preached on this text has this striking title: "A Believer's Last Day His Best Day."[17] Faith can say that our last day in this world is our best day because of what lies ahead of us—we are leaving this world of sin, curse, and death, and bodies that are indwelled by sin and corruption. We will immediately enter a world of holiness, blessing, and life, and we await the resurrection of our bodies in glory. Death is welcome to faith because it introduces us to the life that lies beyond it.

Third, as we think of death and as we think of the life that is ours beyond death, we must think of God in Christ. As Thomas Boston told his congregation, "[We] have a trusty good Friend before [us] in the other world."[18] As wonderful as it is to think of leaving sin, misery, and death behind, and of being reunited with believing loved ones, what makes heaven "heaven" is the presence of Jesus Christ Himself. It is *Christ* who makes heaven the familiar and welcome home that it is to believers. It is because He has "go[ne] to prepare a place for [us]" and will abide there with us that heaven is sweet to the believer (John 14:2). And our Savior is no stranger to the believer. We have communed with Him on earth; we will dwell with Him in heaven. It is the Savior who makes heaven familiar, attractive, delightful, and welcome. Seen in that light, death is Christ's graven message to us that it is time to come home. Warm thoughts of the Savior serve to banish the fears that can accompany death.

So think often of death. Think often of the life and blessedness that lie beyond death for believers. But never think of either life or death without thinking of Christ. And the time to start setting your mind on Christ is . . . right now.

Part Two

ENCOUNTERING DEATH

6

How Do I Face
the Deaths of Others?

We have been thinking about how to *define* death biblically. Now we will think about death in a different light. As Christians, how do we *encounter* death? Death breaks into our lives in a number of ways. We must all prepare for our own deaths (the focus of chapters 8 and 9). We need to learn how to help those who are dying and those who grieve the deaths of loved ones (the focus of chapter 7). And we need to learn for ourselves how to face the deaths of others (the focus of this chapter).

One of the earliest pastoral crises that the Apostle Paul faced did not concern the law of Moses. It did not concern justification by faith alone. It did not concern false teachers in the church. It concerned new believers, recently converted from paganism, who did not know how to face the deaths of their fellow believers. We see from 1 Thessalonians 4:13–18 how Paul helps them—and us—deal with death when it meets them in the loss of believing loved ones.

Encountering Death—Grief

In 1 Thessalonians 4:13, Paul tells believers that we ought "not grieve as others do who have no hope." Paul tells us that there is a biblical way to grieve and an unbiblical way to grieve. Grieving itself is not a sin. We see grief both in biblical example and in biblical command.

The Bible contains multiple examples of believers grieving the deaths of loved ones. Scripture records Jacob as mourning the death (as he believes) of his beloved son Joseph (Gen. 37). In fact, years later, Jacob continues to grieve the loss of Joseph (see 42:36; 43:14). David grieves the death of King Saul and his beloved friend Jonathan (2 Sam. 1). Later, David will grieve the loss of his own son Absalom (2 Sam. 18). In the Gospels, we see Mary and Martha poignantly grieving the death of their brother, Lazarus (John 11). In Acts, the saints in Joppa openly mourn the loss of their sister Dorcas (Acts 9:39). All across redemptive history, then, we see examples of believers grieving the deaths of family and friends.

The Bible also has commands that involve grieving the deaths of others. Paul tells the church in Rome, "Rejoice with those who rejoice, weep with those who weep" (Rom. 12:15). Paul expects us to sympathize in joy and sorrow with all those people whom God has set in our lives, and not only fellow believers.[1] This command therefore applies to the whole range of human relationships in which we find ourselves. The call to "weep" sympathetically captures the fullness of sympathy—emotional, verbal, bodily—that tears of grief express. It is a sin to be indifferent to the grief of a person who is before us. It is both human and Christian to come alongside those who weep and to mourn with them.

In 1 Thessalonians 4:13 Paul assumes that we will grieve in the presence of death. He does not forbid grieving. He only forbids grieving as though we had no hope. We could not fulfill this command to grieve in hope if we did not grieve at all.

So, then, by example and by command, the Bible calls us to grieve the loss of those around us and to mourn with those who grieve the loss of people precious to them. Christians must never be indifferent to death. We are not called to a flinty stoicism. That would be to deny both our humanity and our Christian calling. But Paul does forbid us to grieve as those who grieve without hope. That is a reminder that the gospel transforms our experience of grief. The gospel transforms our thinking, our priorities, our choices, our behaviors, and our inner life generally. It does so not to make us less human but rather to make us the kinds of human beings that God created and redeemed us to be. It is no surprise, then, that the gospel speaks directly to a sad but persistent part of our lives—reckoning with the deaths of the people in our lives.

Grief—Ungodly and Godly

What, then, is the difference between the grief of the ungodly and the grief of the godly? The difference does not lie, we have seen, in grief as such—the profound, often unexpected, even acute sense of sorrow and loss that can affect us, body and soul.[2] The difference lies in the character of that grief. Unbelievers "have no hope," and their mourning reflects that hopelessness. Believers, however, have been given a living hope in Jesus Christ. Our mourning must reflect this gospel hope. Exploring each type of mourning helps us better understand what it means to grieve as those who have hope.

Paul encourages the Ephesians to think back to a time when they were "separated from Christ" (Eph. 2:12). At that time, they "ha[d] no hope and [were] without God in the world" (v. 12). To be without Christ, then, is necessarily to be without hope. To appreciate this connection, it helps to understand what "hope" is. Biblically, hope is the sure expectation of some future benefit not yet possessed.[3] Unlike the hopes that we often have in this world ("I hope it won't rain today"; "I hope my team wins tomorrow"), biblical hopes, since they are connected to the promises that God makes to His people, are certain. But unbelievers have no such hope. They are without any expectation of the promised future benefits that belong only to those who are in Christ.

To be hopeless—to face the future without any expectation of eternal and lasting good—necessarily colors one's experience of grief. For unbelievers, this world is all that they have. They are without God and live for themselves. This lifestyle, Solomon teaches us, is "vanity" (Eccl. 1:2). The pursuit of wisdom, pleasure, labor, and accomplishment in a worldly way all ends up in the same place—"all are from the dust, and to dust all return" (3:20). When death invades the life of a person who is without hope, it is all loss. The lost loved one cannot be retrieved; nor can his death be redeemed. The understandable response is one of despair and hopelessness.

This sense of despair in the presence of death pervaded the gentile world in which the Thessalonian Christians had been reared and were living. Contemporary funerary inscriptions drive home the point.[4] Today, if you walk around a graveyard, you will likely see inscriptions such as the following: "I am the resurrection and the life"; "The Lord is my shepherd"; "Blessed are the dead who die in the Lord." But in the first century, you would see inscriptions such as these: "I was not and I was, I am not and I care not"; "We are nothing. See, reader, how quickly we mortals return from nothing to nothing"; "If you want to know who I am, the answer is ash and burnt embers." These sentiments powerfully express a sense of hopelessness in light of death.

The grief of the godly is marked by a sense of hope, but this hope is not the possession of only some Christians. Every believer has been given hope in the gospel. Each of us has been "born again to a living hope through the resurrection of Jesus Christ from the dead" (1 Peter 1:3). We therefore "rejoice [lit., boast] in hope of the glory of God" (Rom. 5:2). Our hope is not wishful thinking, a strategy to manage or put off the inevitable. It comes from God Himself through the power of the Spirit: "May the God of hope fill you with all joy and peace in believing, so that by the power of the Holy Spirit you may abound in hope" (15:13).

What, then, is our hope? Strictly speaking, our hope is not a *what* but a *who*. It is Christ Himself and all the benefits that we enjoy in Him. Hebrews tells us that we have a "hope that enters into the inner place behind the curtain, where Jesus has gone as a forerunner on our behalf" (Heb. 6:19–20a). Ralph Wardlaw's well-known hymn praises "Christ, of all my hopes the ground." Our hope is in Christ, and our hope is Christ.

In particular, the "blessed hope" of the believer is the "appearing of the glory of our great God and Savior Jesus Christ, who gave himself for us to redeem us from all lawlessness and to purify for himself a people for his own possession who are zealous for good works" (Titus 2:13–14). Our great hope is the return of Christ in glory. Every Christian eagerly awaits the return of Christ and the full experience of eternal life in Him—this is our "blessed hope."

Encourage One Another with These Words

What does this hope look like when we mourn the loss of believing loved ones? How does this hope give us comfort and strength in such times? How can we help our fellow believers to lay hold of this hope in their grief?

Paul's words to the Thessalonians in 1 Thessalonians 4:13–18 answer these questions. While it is difficult to sort out all the details of what was troubling the Thessalonians, the main lines are clear. This is a young church, and many of its members have been recently converted from gentile paganism. Their believing loved ones have died, and they do not know how to respond biblically. Paul is concerned that they will lapse into the familiar cultural response of "griev[ing] as others do who have no hope" (v. 13).

In this passage, Paul applies the truth of the gospel to the Thessalonians' mourning. The gospel does not do away with our grief, but it transforms our grief. Paul is going to explain how that is so. There is a direct, practical component to Paul's teaching. Paul expects the people of the church to "encourage one another with these words" (v. 18). He wants them to take what he says in verses 14–17 and to share these truths as means of comfort to fellow believers in need. This duty does not belong simply to the elders, deacons, or especially mature Christians. It belongs to all believers. We need to gather up the truth of these verses so that we may minister that truth to hurting believers.[5]

Paul offers at least five lines of comfort and encouragement to grieving believers. The first comes in verse 14: "We believe that Jesus died and rose again." Paul here makes three points. First, Jesus has died. In His death, He conquered death. Jesus paid the penalty of sin that merits death, bore the curse of the law on behalf of sinners, and propitiated the wrath of God. Second, Jesus rose again. After three days in the grave, Jesus was raised to newness of life. His body, transformed by the Spirit, is glorious and fit to dwell in heaven. Possessed by the Spirit and possessing the Spirit, our risen Savior shares the Spirit with us, giving blessing, life, and glory to us by the Spirit. Raised from the dead, Jesus gives us every assurance that we will one day be powerfully and gloriously raised from the dead also. Third, Paul reminds us that "we believe"—that Jesus has died and been raised. Paul is saying more than that we assent to these historical facts as facts. We do assent to them, but we have also placed our trust in Christ as Savior and Lord to accomplish the same for us. Our whole lives are lives of faith in Christ, crucified and raised from the dead (2 Cor. 5:7; Gal. 2:20). Because it is true that Jesus died and was raised from the dead, and because we have put our trust in Him as Savior, we have the comfort we need to grieve in hope and to help our brothers and sisters do the same.

The second line of comfort and encouragement is found in 1 Thessalonians 4:16. Believers who have predeceased us are "the dead in Christ."[6] Even in death, the believer remains united to Christ. Death has not destroyed the bond between that person and Jesus Christ. The whole person remains united to Christ—soul and body. His soul has immediately entered the presence of Christ, which is "far better" (Phil. 1:23) than even life in Christ on earth. He has entered his reward and rest. His body rests in his grave as in his bed, awaiting resurrection dawn. Surely our union with Christ affords us great hope and comfort when we mourn the loss of believing loved ones.

Paul's third line traces a timetable of future events. He says that "the dead in Christ will rise first" (1 Thess. 4:16) and that this will happen immediately after the return of Christ ("for the Lord himself will descend from heaven," v. 16). When Christ returns and the dead in Christ are raised, "God will bring with [Jesus] those who have fallen asleep" (v. 14), and "then we who are alive, who are left, will be caught up together with them" (v. 17). Paul assures the Thessalonians that their loved ones who have gone before them in death will not miss out if Christ returns before the Thessalonians join them in death.[7] Nor will they be "second-class" participants in the events surrounding Christ's return. Their resurrection and ingathering to Jesus is the Lord Jesus' first agenda item upon His return (v. 16). If the Thessalonians are alive when Christ returns, they themselves will see their believing loved ones clothed in their glorious resurrection bodies. They will not be looking around and wondering where they may be. These words reassure us that although believers who have died are out of our sight, they very much remain in the mind and heart of Jesus Christ. The events surrounding His return will make that plain.

Fourth, Paul points us to two grand reunions. The first is that believers will then be reunited with dead—now-resurrected—believers: "Then we who are alive, who are left, will be caught up together with them in the clouds" (v. 17). The bodies of believers alive at Christ's return will undergo profound transformation, and the Spirit will make them glorious and in conformity to the resurrection body of Christ (1 Cor. 15:51). They will then be immediately reunited with believers who died before the return of Christ. The second is that all these believers will "meet the Lord in the air" (1 Thess. 4:17). As the Lord appears, we will all appear with Him. What makes these reunions so glorious is that Jesus Christ is at the center of them.

Fifth, Paul reminds us that upon these reunions, "we will always be with the Lord" (v. 17). Jesus does not meet with us and then dismiss us. He gathers us to Himself so that we might be with Him forever. Believers, raised from the dead, along with those believers who were alive at Christ's coming, will dwell forever in the presence of Christ.

These last two lines of consolation make the same point. Death is about separation. Our hope is about reunion. Soul and body will be forever reunited, gloriously. The believing dead and believers who are alive at the second coming will be reunited, and all believers will be gathered to Christ, forever. Our hope reminds us that death is not the final word. In the providence of God, it is one step toward the grand accomplishment and realization of God's purpose to gather His people to Himself in Jesus Christ. This hope cannot but transform our experience of grief. We certainly grieve in view of the tremendous loss that death has brought into our lives, but we grieve in view of the blessings that are sure to come.

Facing the Death of an Unbeliever

We have been thinking about how a believer faces the death of a fellow believer. Clear, certain gospel hope transforms that experience of grief. We are called to minister this hope to our fellow brothers and sisters.

But what if the person who dies is not a believer? Or what if he did not give clear evidence of being a true believer? Believers will and must grieve that death. What does such grief look like?

Compounding a believer's grief in such a situation is that we have no confidence to say that this person has died in Jesus. We therefore have no expectation that the person will be gloriously raised from the dead, reunited with the saints, and brought eternally into the presence of Jesus. We have no expectation that the person is now with the Lord in the way that believers are now with the Lord. How do we face a situation such as this in faith?

We must remember the Bible's teaching that death immediately ushers a person into the presence of the Son of God, who passes sentence and either brings that person into heaven or sends the person to hell (Matt. 25:31–33; John 5:22). The matter is therefore settled. We must not pray for the dead person's salvation.

We must also remember the Bible's teaching that God is perfectly just and righteous. God never does any human being wrong or does injustice (see Gen. 18:25). No one—ourselves included—deserves the least bit of mercy from Him: "He has mercy on whomever he wills" (Rom. 9:18). We must never let our confidence in the integrity of God's character waver.

We should certainly pray in this situation. We should pray that in the midst of a difficult providence, we might find grace from God to submit to His wise will. We should pray that we would rest content in God's purposes, even if we do not fully understand those purposes in a particular situation. We should pray for any living friends or family members of the deceased—that they would find mercy while they are alive, in the only place where sinners may find mercy, in Jesus Christ.

What if someone asks us whether the deceased "is in a better place"? How should we respond? The best thing to do is to steer the conversation toward Jesus Christ and the gospel. As we are able, we should tell the inquirer that hope of eternal life is found in Christ alone and that any sinner who puts his trust in Christ according to the gospel may know that he has been saved by the work of Christ alone. We may not be able to have this conversation right away, and these words, however gently we put them, may not be well received, but sharing the good news about Jesus is the best thing we are able to offer anyone who is grieving.

Conclusion

In this chapter, we have been especially thinking about grieving the death of a loved one from the perspective of the one who is grieving: How do we grieve, in faith, the loss of a fellow believer? How do we help our brothers and sisters in Christ do the same? Put yourself in the shoes of one who, one day, will grieve *your* death. The very best thing that you can do for such a person, the richest inheritance that you can bequeath, is a sound, confirmed, and fruitful profession of faith in Jesus Christ. Let those near and far from you have no doubt or uncertainty that you have gone to be with the Lord.

There are many ways that we can do this. We might have honest, earnest conversations with our friends and family about the root of our confidence in the face of death's approach. We could commit our thoughts to letters or recordings. But one thing we must do is make sure that our lives line up with what we claim to believe. This does not mean, of course, that we come close to living lives of perfection. But it does mean that there is evidence that the grace of Christ has taken up residence in our lives (see Rom. 8:1–11; Gal. 5:22–23).

Whether you are serving your loved ones by preparing them for your death or whether you are grieving the loss of a fellow believer, you need the same thing: the gospel of Christ. This means that we need to commit to hearing the gospel preached every Lord's Day. It means that we are spending time with fellow Christians to encourage one another in faith and godliness. It means that we are regularly spending time in the prayerful study of, meditation on, and application of Scripture. Preparation for death never begins at death—whether someone else's or the imminent arrival of our own. Preparation for death begins right now by drawing close to Jesus Christ and finding grace in Him to face death and to encourage others who will face death.

7

How Do I Help
the Dying and Grieving?

I n the previous chapter, we thought about how the Christian should face
the deaths of others, particularly believers. For those who die in the Lord,
Paul tells us, we are to grieve, but we are to grieve in hope. The good news that
Jesus Christ has died and been raised from the dead for sinners transforms our
experience of grief.

Now we are going to think about how the Bible guides us in helping others who are facing death. First, we will think about what counsel Scripture
gives us for ministering to those who are dying. Second, we will think about
some biblical principles to guide us as we reach out to those who are grieving
the loss of loved ones.

Ministering to the Dying

Sometimes death comes suddenly and unexpectedly—a heart attack or an
automobile accident, for example. But often people know that death is rapidly
approaching. How can we as Christians reach out and serve the people in our
lives who know that they are close to death? We may answer that question
from Scripture along five lines.

Preparation

The first thing we should do, before we step in to help those who are dying,
is to prepare ourselves in at least two ways. First, we should equip ourselves
with Scripture's teaching on death and dying, the gospel, and the way that the

gospel offers hope to dying people. We never know what kinds of questions or conversations may arise. We want to be ready to speak a good and profitable word when we have the opportunity. We also want to be sure that we are sensitive to the circumstances of the person whom we are visiting. Is the person weak or weary? Is he discouraged? Does his condition (or prescribed medications) impair his ability to think clearly or to carry on a conversation? Paul tells us that our speech must be "such . . . as fits the occasion" (Eph. 4:29). We want to be sure that the words we choose and the length of our visit help and do not burden the person whom we want to serve.

Second, we should prepare ourselves spiritually for what we could see. It may be that our friend or loved one has undergone significant physical changes since we last saw him. It may be that he is showing evident mental decline or impairment. Especially at such times, we should remember what the Bible teaches about the human person. The soul is distinct from the body.[1] If a believer has experienced noticeable physical or mental deterioration, that does not mean that the person has undergone spiritual decay or decline. In fact, as Paul reminds us, "we do not lose heart. Though our outer self is wasting away, our inner self is being renewed day by day" (2 Cor. 4:16). The believer may well be growing and flourishing spiritually even as his body is withering and preparing to die. We should also remember what Paul told the Colossians: "Your life is hidden with Christ in God" (Col. 3:3). The believer's "life" in Christ is secure in the Savior. The ravages of injury and disease cannot touch that life.

Presence

The second thing we can do to serve those who are dying is to be ready simply to "be there." When we come to a dying person's bedside, we may feel immense pressures. Our visit may have to be a short one. We may never see the person again in this life. There are important things that we want to share with him and ask him. We struggle to find the right words to say. When we sense the weight of doing just the right thing, it is important to remember that the best thing to do may be to say little or nothing at all.

When Job's friends first visited him, they were at first overwhelmed at the sight of his suffering (see Job 2:12). Scripture records that "they sat with him on the ground seven days and seven nights, and no one spoke a word to him, for they saw that his suffering was very great" (2:13). Perhaps the very best thing that they did was to be with Job and to say nothing. It was when they began to speak to Job that trouble began (see 42:7–9). Job himself recognized this. He pronounced his friends "worthless" counselors and said to them, "Oh that you would keep silent, and it would be your wisdom!" (13:4–5). They ceased comforting when they started speaking!

This is not to say that we should not say anything when we are with someone who is dying. It is to say that even when we speak sparingly (or not at all), we can still minister comfort to the person. Simply being there, holding the person's hand or squeezing his shoulder, is a powerful expression of love.

When we do speak to the person, we can say many things. We can read portions of Scripture that point him to Christ and that minister comfort to the believing soul—Psalm 23 and Romans 8, to take only two examples. We can sing a favorite hymn. We can pray with or for the person. If we do take the opportunity to speak with him, our aim should be "listen, don't solve."[2] In other words, our calling is not to resolve every theological question that arises from the circumstances of our sick friend or loved one. Our calling is to share the Word of God with the person in ways that are understandable and meaningful to his life and situation.

What if the one we visit is unresponsive? Though the person cannot communicate with us, he may yet be able to hear what we say. We should assume that the person can understand everything that we say in his presence. Read Scripture to him. Sing biblical hymns to him. Pray audibly for him. Who knows how the Spirit may use the Word of God in effective and unseen ways in the life of this sick person?

It is often very difficult to enter a hospital, a nursing home, or hospice care and to see someone we know and love reduced and laid low by disease. A part of us may simply want to avoid going at all. At such times, we should remember what Paul tells the Galatians: "Bear one another's burdens, and so fulfill the law of Christ" (Gal. 6:2). Loving others is frequently costly.[3] In this case, to show Christian love to one in need is a genuine "burden" for us to bear. That is when we pray for strengthening grace, exercise self-denial, and commit to putting our friend's needs before our own. Paul himself followed this pattern. Writing to the Corinthians, he reminded them that when he first preached the gospel to them, "[he] was with [them] in weakness and in fear and much trembling" (1 Cor. 2:3). It was a hard thing for Paul to preach Christ to the Corinthians. But it was something that he had to do (see 9:16). And the Lord, in time, brought much fruit from that difficult act of obedience. We, too, may see eternal good come out of these small but difficult expressions of Christian love to those in need.

Prognosis

The third thing that we should do to minister well to those who are dying is to respect the medical prognosis. The doctors may well conclude that there is little likelihood of survival. They may prescribe a course of palliative care—to make the patient comfortable but not to heal him of his disease or condition. The illness will be allowed to move toward its inevitable and unpreventable end, death.

It is not sinful to acknowledge that in God's providence, this person is nearing death. It is not sinful to recognize that death cannot be avoided in this situation. If the body is preparing to die, we should not evade or vainly forestall that outcome. To be sure, we must never kill someone who is dying. But we may allow someone who is dying to close his days in dignity and in comfort. We do this in humble recognition that we are limited creatures and that we all, in the providence of God, must die.[4]

Sometimes Christians will ask: "Shouldn't we pray for miraculous healing? Isn't it faithless *not* to expect that God will restore life to someone who is at the brink of death? Doesn't James 5:15 say that 'the prayer of faith will save the one who is sick, and the Lord will raise him up'?"

These questions raise important issues, and we should think about them carefully. In the first place, we wholeheartedly affirm that God is able to do anything that is consistent with His character and that we must believe every promise that He has made to us. The question is not whether God is *able* to heal this sick person or that sick person but whether God has pledged Himself to heal every sick person for whom the elders pray in faith.[5] We have no right to demand of God something that He has not committed Himself to do. We may only expect Him to do what He has told us in the Bible that He will do.

When we look at James 5:15 in the context of James' teaching as a whole, it is mistaken to conclude that he is teaching that God will bring healing to everyone for whom the prayer of faith is made. It is no less mistaken to infer that if a believer dies of his illness, the elders praying for him failed to pray with sufficient faith.

Three considerations from James' letter confirm these conclusions and help us see what James *is* telling us here. First, in the previous chapter, James has admonished those who engage in business pursuits and say, "Today or tomorrow we will go into such and such a town and spend a year there and trade and make a profit" (James 4:13). This attitude, James warns, is sheer presumption: "You do not know what tomorrow will bring. . . . Instead you ought to say, 'If the Lord wills, we will live and do this or that'" (vv. 14–15). This principle applies no less to prayer than it does to the marketplace. Our prayers should always recognize that our requests are subject to the Lord's eternal and unchangeable decree. When we pray for a sick brother or sister's recovery, it may be that the Lord will heal the person, but He may not.

Second, James reminds us at the outset of the letter that no believer is spared troubles or trials. "Trials" are the "testing of [our] faith," which "produces steadfastness," in order that we may be "perfect and complete, lacking in nothing." Thus, we must "count it all joy . . . when [we] meet trials of various kinds" (1:2–4). Trials certainly include sickness, even mortal sickness. If God has purposed that a believer fall ill and die from that illness, His intention in that sickness is to bring spiritual growth and health to that believer. If God does not remove that illness, and if God brings about this believer's death from that illness, God's purpose is only good toward him.

Third, James gives us two Old Testament examples that illuminate what he is talking about in James 5:15. Just a few verses earlier, James has pointed us to the "steadfastness of Job" and "the purpose of the Lord, how the Lord is compassionate and merciful" (v. 11). Job suffered mightily and felt, at points, near death. His suffering was not the result of his faithlessness or disobedience. Quite the contrary (see Job 1:6–12; 2:1–6). Nor was God forsaking Job. He had appointed this trial for His own glory and for the ultimate good of His servant Job.

Immediately after James 5:15, James points us to the example of Elijah: "The prayer of a righteous person has great power as it is working. Elijah . . . prayed fervently that it might not rain, and for three years and six months it did not rain on the earth. Then he prayed again, and heaven gave rain, and the earth bore its fruit" (vv. 16–18). As Sinclair Ferguson reminds us, Elijah is "taking God's covenant promise of judgement back to him in prayer and asking him to fulfill it . . . (Deut. 11:16–17; compare 28:15, 23)."[6] Thus, "the 'prayer of faith' then is not something that we work up from within. Rather it is our bringing God's promises back to him, asking him to keep them, and trusting him that he will."[7]

In summary, James is telling us that when a believer is sick, he should call the elders to pray over him. The elders must pray in submission to God's decree— "if the Lord wills" (compare 1 Sam. 3:18). They must not pray presumptively but are to pray as they lay hold of the promises that God has made in Scripture, trusting that He will make good on those promises in His own manner and time. The believer should recognize that this trial has not come about by chance or accident. It is the Lord's purpose to work spiritual good in the Christian's life. He has the biblical example of Job to encourage him in this respect.

What, then, does James mean when he says that "the prayer of faith *will save the one who is sick, and the Lord will raise him up*" (James 5:15, emphasis added)? It may be that the Lord will grant healing to that brother or sister, but it may be that the person will die. What, then, of James' words? How is this believer "save[d]" or "raise[d] up"? The believer who dies goes immediately into the presence of the Lord and awaits the ultimate and complete salvation and healing—the reunion of his glorified resurrected body with his (now) perfected soul.[8] In either case—restoration to health or entry through death into the presence of Christ—the Lord has made good on His promise, according to His good purpose.

Point to Christ

The fourth thing that we should do to help those who are dying is to find ways to point them to Christ. When his thirteen-year-old daughter, Magdalena, lay dying, Martin Luther came to her bedside to speak with her. Luther was in the deep distress of a father preparing to lose his beloved daughter. In that distress, he wanted to help Magdalena think about God in Christ in her final hours on earth. "Magdalena, my little daughter, you would gladly remain here with me, your father. Are you also glad to go to your Father in heaven?" She answered, "Yes, dear father, as God will."[9]

We should want to do the same thing that Martin Luther did with Magdalena. While we should not be reckless in what we say to those who are dying, we should not be timid either. These may be some of our final conversations that we have with them in this world. These moments are solemn, and we should try to use them to speak of eternal things.

One way that we can do this is to ask open-ended questions: "What are you thinking about these days?" "Do you have any fears or worries?" "Is there anything that you would like to say while I am with you?"

If the person we are visiting is an unbeliever, then we know from Scripture that certain things are true about him. We know that he has objective guilt before God for his sin. We know that he fears the punishment that he deserves and will receive after death. We know that he is relying on all the wrong things if he hopes to be accepted by God—his good works, his good intentions, his church membership (if he has one), and so on. In such a situation, we want to share the good news with the person, briefly, simply, and pointedly. Tell him that sin is real and rightly deserves the eternal punishment of God. Tell him that no sinner can stand righteous in himself before God. Tell him that Christ lived, died, and rose again to bring sinners near to God. Explain the way of justification—that Christ took sinners' sins on the cross; that through faith in Christ, Christ's righteousness is imputed or counted to the sinner; that on the basis of Christ's imputed righteousness alone, the sinner is counted righteous in God's sight. Tell the person that Christ has won the victory over death and entry into eternal life for all who trust Him. If we leave the dying person with the gospel, then we have pointed him to a haven in the storm. Who knows what God may do through His Word in those final hours and days of this person's life?

If the person we are visiting is a professing believer, then we should help him to meet the spiritual challenges that he may face in death's approach. In John Bunyan's *Pilgrim's Progress*, Christian will die by crossing a great river. As he does so, he begins to sink in the waters and to despair. His pilgrim friend, Hopeful, encourages him with gospel truth. A believer, as death approaches, may expect to be assaulted by devils and by his own flesh. The discomfort, pain, and distress attending death may cloud the believer's view of Christ and His grace.

At such times, it is our privilege to point the person to the gospel that he professes to believe. We remind him of the sovereign love of our heavenly Father, a love that will never let him go. We remind him of the sufficiency of

Christ's work to bring him near to God and to keep him there. We remind the believer of the invincible and preserving power and the comforting presence of the Holy Spirit, who is his in Christ. We remind him that Christ has gone before him in death into heaven, and that He will be with him all the way to deliver him to his heavenly home.

Prayer

Finally, we minister to those who are dying by praying with and for them. Prayer should suffuse the entirety of our service to a sick and dying person— our preparations to see him, our visits to him, and the biblical counsel we give him. What are some ways that we may pray for him?

First, we should pray that the person would have a sure and settled faith in Jesus Christ. About a month before he died, an ailing John Calvin told fellow ministers who were visiting him that "my faults have always displeased me and the root of the fear of the Lord has always been in my heart."[10] Calvin was well acquainted with his sins. For that reason, he took refuge in the Lord, trusting and fearing Him from the heart. We should pray that our dying friend or loved one would, by God's grace, make the same kind of confession.

Second, we should pray that the person would submit himself to the will of God. If it is evident in God's providence that his time on this earth is limited, then the best thing to do is to bow before God. We should also pray for ourselves that we would submit to this hard providence. We may pray this prayer for the dying person and for ourselves in confidence that God is working only for His glory and the good of His people in this world (Rom. 8:28). We trust God even when we do not fully understand what He is doing in our lives.

Third, we should pray that our dying loved one would have comfort of body and soul. We do not want him to linger in physical pain. It is not necessarily wrong to pray that the Lord would take a dying believer home to Him soon. We also do not want the person to experience distress of soul. We should pray that he would experience the "peace of God, which surpasses all understanding" and "guard[s]" "hearts" and "minds in Christ Jesus" (Phil. 4:7).

Finally, we should pray that God would provide for the family and friends whom the dying person will leave behind. Pray that He would fulfill His promise to watch over the widow and the orphan (Deut. 10:18; Ps. 68:5).

Pray that He would spiritually provide for the survivors as they grieve their loss, that their grief may be in the hope of the gospel.

Ministering to the Grieving

As we pray for the friends and family of a loved one whom they have lost in death, we should take the opportunity to serve them in other ways as well. There are many things that we may do, but there are three in particular.

Step Forward

The first thing that we should do is step forward to help. The experience of grieving and mourning is an overwhelming one—emotionally, physically, and otherwise. Sometimes it can paralyze mourners in their tracks. And this can happen at a time when many decisions must be made in a relatively short time—funeral arrangements and settling of finances, to name just two.

While we do not want to be in the way of the family as they grieve together, there are ways that we can unobtrusively offer concrete help to them. It can be as simple as a brief phone call or a text message. We can visit them. We can bring them a meal. We can offer transportation or housing to family members who have traveled from out of town.

We shouldn't wait for them to ask us for help (they probably won't). Nor should we assume that the church elders and deacons will take care of everything. Good elders and deacons work hard, and much of their work is quiet and behind the scenes. But no session or board of deacons—as good as they are—can be everywhere or can do everything. There will always be more to do. There will always be opportunities for you and me to step forward and lend a helping hand to those in need.

Serve for the Long Haul

Grieving and mourning does not end right after the funeral. Your life may return to normal when you return home from the service, but the family's lives do not. They will grieve and have special needs in the months and years ahead. We should think of ways to serve them over a long period. Ways to serve include (but are not limited to) regular (but not obtrusive) phone calls or texts; handwritten cards or notes sent through the mail; invitations to coffee or meals; remembrances of (as appropriate) the deceased person's birthday and the day of his death; and sensitivity on holidays to those who have lost loved ones.[11] You cannot anticipate or overestimate how much the seemingly smallest gesture can mean to a still-grieving person.

Speak of the Deceased

This third way of serving those who are grieving may seem counterintuitive. Wouldn't talking to friends and family members about their lost loved one only open fresh wounds? While we cannot underscore enough the importance of being sensitive in the way that we have these discussions, the opposite is often the case—having these conversations does not harm but helps the bereaved. You might think of anecdotes or stories that are personal, perhaps incidents that the family or close friends never witnessed or saw for themselves. Think of encouraging words, acts of service, or demonstrations of character that you saw in the deceased person's life. Express appropriately your indebtedness to him and your gratitude to God for him. Above all, if the deceased person was a believer, be sure to testify—honestly and sincerely—to his faith in Christ and to the fruit of his faith. Approaching mourning friends and family with these remembrances can be a powerful witness to an unbelieving mourner and a tremendous comfort to a believing mourner.

What about Suicide?

Finally, in closing, what if the deceased has died by suicide? Death is tragic enough, and suicide compounds that tragedy. How should we think biblically about suicide, and how should we extend comfort to the friends and family members of someone who has taken his own life? We may offer three observations.

First, suicide, the deliberate taking of one's own life, is a sin against the sixth commandment, "You shall not murder" (Ex. 20:13). We typically think of this commandment in terms of the unjust taking of another's life. It applies no less, however, to our own lives. To take our own lives is to sin against the God who made us and owns us. God has not allowed us to end our lives whenever we want (see Jer. 10:23). The few examples of suicide that we find in Scripture do not commend the practice. King Saul, Ahithophel, and Judas Iscariot took their own lives and died in shame. When the Apostle Paul saw the Philippian jailer about to take his own life, he pleaded with him not to carry out his intention (Acts 16:28). Suicide finds no support in Scripture, whether from command or from example. On the contrary, Scripture forbids suicide.

People take their lives for all sorts of reasons, and often there are mitigating factors or considerations. Substance abuse or mental illness might have affected one's judgment. A powerful fear of consequences for bad choices made might have been at play. Circumstances such as the loss of a job or the ending of a relationship might have overwhelmed a person. Furthermore, a person who succeeds in taking his life might not have done so with complete resolve.

While these factors help us better understand the person who tries to take or succeeds in taking his own life, they do not change the fact that suicide is a violation of God's law. Taking one's own life is never the right thing to do. It does not please God.

Second, suicide is not an unpardonable sin. When Jesus identified a single unpardonable sin, it was not suicide (Matt. 12:31; Luke 12:10).[12] There is therefore no absolute bar to the pardon of suicide. If a professing Christian were to take his own life, his suicide would not require us to say that he was not a Christian. To be sure, the manner of his death leaves a cloud on his profession and reputation and raises many unsettling questions among his friends and family. But it does not of itself exclude him from the kingdom. Jesus died for all the sins of His people, including the sin of suicide.[13] This fact in no way justifies a believer's attempt to take his own life. But it does offer genuine comfort to those who mourn the loss of someone who dies by suicide.

Third, among those who mourn the loss of someone who has died by suicide, there may be and often is a host of feelings—shame, resentment, anger, and guilt—toward the deceased. Anger is certainly understandable, even justifiable—suicide is profoundly selfish and thoughtless. But to nurture these feelings is to drink spiritual poison. To those mourners who are experiencing the turmoil that comes in the wake of the news of a death by suicide, the best thing that we can offer is the good news of Christ. They need the peace and the comfort that Christ offers to us in the gospel. They also need to heed the call of Christ to be willing to forgive from the heart the person who has sinned against them by taking his own life. That is to say, they need what every other mourning person needs—indeed, what every human being needs. We need Christ.

8

How Do I Prepare for Death? (Part 1)

In the previous two chapters, we have thought about how the Bible guides us in responding to death. When our fellow believers die, we are to grieve in hope. When unbelievers die, we rest in the sovereignty of God and point others to Christ. When our brothers and sisters in Christ are preparing to die or are grieving the loss of a loved one, we have a calling to serve them.

Now we will think about how to prepare ourselves for death. Because this is such a wide-ranging and important topic, we will devote two chapters to it. In the next chapter, we will reflect on the this-worldly preparations that we should make for death—preparing our family and our estate; making plans for our funeral and burial; and getting a handle on some of the end-of-life questions that we may have to answer. In this chapter, we are thinking about the spiritual preparations for death that believers should be making. Death is real and, barring the return of Christ, is inevitable for us all. How do we prepare for this certainty, even and especially when death seems distant and remote from us? We may trace five lines of counsel from Scripture that show us how God wants us to be preparing for death.

Attend to the Means of Grace

First, God calls us to set apart the Lord's Day as a day of worship and holy resting. God set this pattern for us in the creation. After making the world and everything in it within the space of six days, God "rested on the seventh day from all his work that he had done. So God blessed the seventh day and made it holy, because on it God rested from all his work that he had done in creation" (Gen. 2:2b–3). God has given the Sabbath to all people as a day to "rest" from all their labors on the other six days and to dedicate this "holy" day to God's worship. God confirmed this command in the Ten Commandments that He gave to Israel on Mount Sinai (Ex. 20:8–11; Deut. 5:12–15).[1]

With the resurrection of Christ, the Sabbath command remained in place, but the particular day changed.[2] The church, under the direction and supervision of Christ's Apostles, gathered for worship on the *first* day of the week (Acts 20:7; 1 Cor. 16:2), a day that the Apostle John calls "the Lord's day" (Rev. 1:10). The reason for this change of day is that Christ was raised from the dead on the first day of the week (Matt. 28:1; Mark 16:2; Luke 24:1; John 20:1; compare John 20:19, 26). God set apart the seventh day of the week to commemorate the accomplished work of creation. He now sets apart the first day to commemorate the accomplished work of new creation.

The letter to the Hebrews tells us that there is a connection between the Lord's Day and eternal life. God's new covenant people are in the same place that Israel was in the wilderness—between Egypt and Canaan. In the wilderness, we are making our way toward the "rest" that God has promised to us in Christ (Heb. 4:1–2). We will enter this rest by faith in the gospel (vv. 2–3). This faith is active in resisting the sin that tempts us (3:13; 4:11) and in producing good works that are pleasing to God (4:10). This rest is something that we have yet to enter—"there remains a Sabbath rest for the people of God" (v. 9).[3] Notice here that Hebrews calls this future rest a "*Sabbath* rest." This description tells us at least two things. First, heaven is an eternal Sabbath, when we will rest from our labors on earth and delight in the worship of the triune God. Second, by implication, every weekly Sabbath is a pointer toward this eternal Sabbath. Each Lord's Day, we are not only remembering what God has done for us in Jesus Christ but also looking forward to our heavenly home. We are currently pilgrims and on the way. We are not there yet. But we will arrive there by the grace and power of our faithful God.

When we are obedient to God's call to worship Him weekly on the Lord's Day, we remind ourselves and others that God has prepared a heavenly rest for us. Moreover, God has designed public worship to help us think more about that rest and to live in this world in light of that rest. The center of God's worship is the reading and preaching of the Word of God. A ministry that is faithful to the Word of God will, over time, regularly remind us of our sin and misery, of the gospel of grace, and of the hope of eternal life in Christ.

This is one reason that it is critical that we gather, week after week, with the church in the worship of God. Just as we need a regular, balanced diet of wholesome food to maintain good bodily health, we need a regular, balanced diet of the Word of God to maintain spiritual health. The ministry of the Word will provide spiritual nourishment that, received through faith, will equip us to keep on in our pilgrimage. One way that it does this is by reminding us of the rest that lies ahead of us and of the joys that await us there.

Commune Often with God in Christ

A second way to be preparing ourselves for death is to commune often with God in Jesus Christ. Paul told the Philippians, "For to me to live is Christ, and to die is gain" (Phil. 1:21). Death is most certainly gain to every believer. What gave Paul the confidence to say that? It is that, for Paul as he is writing, "to live is Christ." What does it mean, "to live is Christ"? It means that we live in union with Christ and, united to Him, in fellowship with God the Father, Son, and Holy Spirit. Union and communion with Christ touch on every aspect of the Christian life. It is for that reason critical that we prepare ourselves for death. The Puritan Edward Pearse exhorts us, "Get into Christ, get union with Christ, and an interest in Christ by believing . . . to fit and prepare [you] for a dying hour."[4]

We may look at two passages that help us better understand what Paul meant by "to live is Christ." The first is Galatians 2:20: "I have been crucified with Christ. It is no longer I who live, but Christ who lives in me. And the life I now live in the flesh I live by faith in the Son of God, who loved me and gave himself for me." Here Paul reminds us that each believer is united with Christ—we have been "crucified with Christ" and "Christ . . . lives in me." I am in Christ, and Christ is in me.

Paul further explains this reality along two lines. The first is that of *death*—we have been "crucified with Christ," and "it is no longer I who live." What does Paul mean by that statement? He goes on to say that "I now live." So how can Paul "no longer . . . live" and "now live" at the same time? When

Paul says, "It is no longer I who live," he is speaking of who he used to be, apart from Jesus Christ. This is Paul-in-Adam (see Rom. 5:12–21). *This* Paul has been nailed to the cross. All things are now new (2 Cor. 5:17). He has a new relationship to the flesh—that is, his former life in sin (Gal. 5:24). He has a new relationship to the world, and the world has a new relationship to him (6:14). He has a new relationship to the law of God and to God Himself (2:16; 3:14). The cross has changed everything for Paul.

The second line is that of *life*: "It is no longer I who live, but Christ who lives in me. And the life I now live in the flesh I live by faith in the Son of God" (Gal. 2:20). The old "I" has been nailed to the cross—he no longer determines Paul's existence. It is Christ who determines Paul's existence. Christ is the principle of life in Paul. Paul is very much alive—he "now live[s] in the flesh." Christ doesn't live this life for Paul or in the place of Paul. Rather, Paul now lives by the gracious power of the indwelling Christ. The way that Paul experiences this new life is through "faith." Faith colors every dimension of Paul's life. As he tells the Corinthians, "We walk by faith, not by sight" (2 Cor. 5:7).[5] This faith is not faith in faith or faith in Paul's own abilities and powers. It is faith in the Son of God, who gave Himself in love for Paul at the cross.

A second passage that helps us understand what Paul means by "to live is Christ" is Romans 8:1–11. Here we see some of the same ideas and words that Paul uses in Galatians 2:20.[6] Paul helps us see that life in Christ is a life lived in the Spirit. For Christ to be in us (Rom. 8:10) is for the Spirit to dwell in us (v. 9)—that is, the Spirit of Christ (8:9), "the Spirit of him who raised Jesus from the dead" (v. 11).

How should we think about the indwelling of the Spirit? Paul helps us to see the evidence and fruit of His abiding presence in our lives. If the Spirit indwells us, Paul argues, then we "set [our] minds on the things of the Spirit" (Rom. 8:5). There is a mindset of the Holy Spirit—altogether different from that of the "flesh" (sin). How do we access the mind of the Spirit? Paul elsewhere directs us to the book that the Spirit wrote, the Bible (see 2 Tim. 3:16: "All Scripture is breathed out by God"). The Spirit penned the Bible so that we would have a complete and sufficient record of what He wants us to know for faith and practice.

And since the Spirit indwells us, we will have not only a mindset shaped and governed by the Spirit but a lifestyle directed by and pleasing to the Spirit. We must "walk not according to the flesh but according to the Spirit" (Rom. 8:4). As Paul writes to the Galatians, "If we live by the Spirit, let us also keep in step with the Spirit" (Gal. 5:25). We obey these commands by following all the commands that God the Spirit, in Scripture, gives to us.

In summary, to be in union and communion with Jesus Christ means that we are united to Christ and that Christ indwells us. We believe in Christ as He is offered to us in the gospel, and we keep on believing. When we get Christ, we necessarily get the Spirit as well. To live in the Spirit is to pursue a mindset that is conformed to the Spirit's mind revealed in Scripture and a lifestyle in keeping with the pattern of life given to us in the Bible.

What does this have to do with preparing for death? Everything! Paul tells the Romans that since God in the power of the Spirit "raised Jesus from the dead," then "he who raised Christ Jesus from the dead will also give life to your mortal bodies through his Spirit who dwells in you" (Rom. 8:11). We have assurance that if the Spirit is at work in us *now*, He will most certainly be at work in us *then*—to raise us from the dead in glorious conformity to the resurrection body of Christ (Phil. 3:21). The Spirit is changing us from the inside out. Right now, His work is invisible and secret, but no less real. Our bodies are undergoing outward decay, but the Spirit is renewing us inwardly, day by day (2 Cor. 4:16). The crown and capstone of the Spirit's work of renewal in our lives is the bodily resurrection. The comfort and assurance that we have currently is that God always finishes what He starts (Phil. 1:6). If the Spirit is at work in our lives now, He will see that work right through to its conclusion.

This reality means that the more we strive to live the kind of life that Paul lays out for us in Galatians 2:20 and Romans 8:1–11, the more comfort and assurance we have of our gospel hope in the face of death. This life pattern in no way earns or merits anything from God, much less life after death. Our sole title to eternal life is the justifying righteousness of Christ, imputed to us and received through faith alone (Rom. 5:17). This life pattern, rather, is the way that we know that the Spirit is present and at work in our lives.[7] Pursuing this pattern is the God-assigned pathway to enjoying the blessings of gospel hope that are ours in Jesus Christ. The best way to get ready for death is to live—in, by, and for Jesus Christ.

Enjoy Fellowship with God's People

The third thing that we can do to prepare ourselves for death is to enjoy fellowship with the people of God. We have been thinking of preparing for death thus far in largely individual terms. But preparing for death is not individualistic. We are pilgrims traveling to our heavenly home in company with the people of God (Heb. 3:7–4:13). We are united to Christ and thereby united to and in fellowship with the body of believers (1 Cor. 12:12–13). Preparing ourselves for death means living in fellowship with the church of God.

This is the point that the writer to the Hebrews makes toward the end of his letter: "And let us consider how to stir up one another to love and good works, not neglecting to meet together, as is the habit of some, but encouraging one another, and all the more as you see the Day drawing near" (Heb. 10:24–25).

Looming over these commands is the fact that "the Day" of Christ's return is "drawing near" (Heb. 10:24–25). This day is one for which every believer longs (1 Cor. 16:22), for on that day we will obtain "the outcome of [our] faith, the salvation of [our] souls" (1 Peter 1:9). This day is "drawing near." As Paul reminds us, "Salvation is nearer to us now than when we first believed" (Rom. 13:11).

In light of this approaching day, how do we live? The writer says that we are to provoke one another! Not to exasperation, but "to love and good works" (Heb. 10:24). We encourage one another to abound in the fruit of the Spirit. When we do this, we are helping our brothers and sisters in Christ to have a well-grounded hope in Christ and the fullness of life that He will give to His people when He returns in glory.

The writer then tells us not to neglect "to meet together, as is the habit of some" (Heb. 10:25). The time to encourage one another is when we gather together, regularly, on the Lord's Day.[8] This mutual encouragement takes place in public worship and before and after it, when believers spend time with one another in Christian fellowship.

As Hebrews reminds us earlier in the letter, it is hard work to be a pilgrim. Perhaps you can think of an arduous, difficult journey or trip that you have made. You know from experience how much easier it is to bear the hardships and disappointments of travel when you are traveling with family or friends. In the same way, God calls us to undertake our pilgrimage to heaven together.

As the day approaches, we band together to encourage one another along the way. That doesn't mean that the trip will be easy or free of problems, but it does mean that God is providing a way to ease the burdens of the journey. And it also whets our appetites for our heavenly home. The life that God calls us to live in preparation for death is a life lived together with God's people.

Hold This World Loosely

The fourth way that we can prepare for death is to learn more and more to hold this world loosely. A big part of what prompts fear in the face of death is that we will have to part from this world—all that is familiar to us, and particularly our families and our fellow believers. To be sure, this loss is real. The Bible, however, wants us to keep a couple of things in mind as we prepare to leave this world in death.

The first is that, as believers, we have a new relationship with the world. To understand this new relationship, we should remember that the Bible speaks of the "world" in a couple of different ways. Its most basic sense is the sum total of what God has created—heaven and earth and everything in them. In this respect, the world is only good and we are to receive and use the things of this world in thanksgiving (see 1 Tim. 4:3–4).

But the Bible speaks of "world" in another distinct sense. This sense captures the world as we currently experience it. It is the world as it lies under the curse of God, subject to futility and in bondage to corruption (Rom. 8:20–21). It is the world considered as the mass of humanity in rebellion against God and committed to sin and unrighteousness (see 1 John 2:16–17).

In Christ, we have a new relationship to the world, considered in this last sense (see John 17:16). "The world has been crucified to me," Paul tells the Galatians, "and I to the world" (Gal. 6:14). This is true because Jesus has "overcome the world" (John 16:33), and therefore, "everyone who has been born of God overcomes the world. And this is the victory that has overcome the world—our faith" (1 John 5:4).

As believers, we don't belong to the world, so defined, because we have "citizenship . . . in heaven" (Phil. 3:20). Like Abraham, Isaac, and Jacob, we are "strangers and exiles on the earth" who "desire a better country, that is, a heavenly one" (Heb. 11:13, 16). While it is hard to leave this world in some ways (parting with our family, our friends, our fellow believers), it should not be hard to leave this world in other ways. We are leaving a world that is marred by sin, rebellion, and the curse. Think of how often the world has hindered—and certainly not helped—your fellowship with God, your service to God, and your love for Him (see Luke 21:34). Thomas Boston spoke pointedly to his congregation along these lines: "While you live here, you sin, and see others sinning. You breathe infectious air. You live in a pest house."[9] It is never a grief or burden to think that one day we will set this behind us once and for all.

A second thing to keep in mind is the impermanence of this world. Paul reminds the Corinthians that "the appointed time has grown very short. From now on, let those who have wives live as though they had none . . . and those who deal with the world as though they had no dealings with it. For the present form of this world is passing away" (1 Cor. 7:29, 31). As believers, we are awaiting the return of Christ, the consummation of all things, new heavens and a new earth. We will "receiv[e] a kingdom that cannot be shaken" (Heb. 12:28). The new creation is lasting and permanent. The present order of things is "passing away" and subject to being "shaken" (12:26–27). This was true even in the garden. God made Adam alive, in fellowship with Him. But this life was one that Adam could—and did—lose. If Adam had obeyed God, he would have entered into confirmed fellowship with God, a life that he could not lose (Gen. 2:16).[10] Adam failed to do this, but the last Adam has accomplished this in His death and resurrection, and He freely gives us this life through faith in Him (Rom. 6:23; see 5:12–21).

This world—even at its best—was never designed to be permanent. God made it to find its realization in the God-man, Christ Jesus. God achieved this goal in and by the death and resurrection of Christ (Eph. 1:10). As tragic as death is, and as sad as it is to leave all that is familiar, we should remember that God has better things in store for us. Death is the way that God brings His people to enjoy more and more the riches and blessings of the new creation.

Think Often of Heaven

This leads to a fifth and final way to be preparing ourselves spiritually for death. Not only should we have a clear-eyed view of what this world is, but we should also have a strong grasp of the world that awaits us. The reason that we may and must do so is that in Christ we already belong to that world: "Our citizenship is in heaven" (Phil. 3:20). "For here we have no lasting city, but we seek the city that is to come" (Heb. 13:14). "Therefore let us be grateful for receiving a kingdom that cannot be shaken" (12:28). Heaven is ours even if we are not yet in heaven.

One way to think about heaven is to compare it with our current lives. We may explore five such points of comparison to help us long for what awaits us. First, as we have seen, we are currently on pilgrimage. We are "striv[ing] to enter [the] rest" that is ours in Christ (4:11; compare v. 9). There will come a day when we will rest "from [our] works as God did from his" (v. 10; compare v. 4, which quotes Gen. 2:3). This will be a blessed state: "'Blessed are the dead who die in the Lord from now on.' 'Blessed indeed,' says the Spirit, 'that they may rest from their labors, for their deeds follow them!'" (Rev. 14:13). This world is, for us, one of striving and toil. Heaven will be a place of rest and refreshment.

Second, we live in a world that is marked by corruption and death because of sin. In Christ, we have begun to experience resurrection life (Eph. 2:4–10). The believer's death is, for him, "gain" (Phil. 1:21). We will experience life in Christ to a degree that we have never experienced in this world. No more curse, corruption, sin, misery, or death. Not even the threat of these things. Only and always blessing, glory, joy, righteousness, and life.

Third, this world is characterized by uncertainty and loss. Whether it is property, possessions, health, or the people we love, we live every day knowing that we could lose any of them in an instant. And that threat of loss lessens our enjoyment of them. But the "inheritance" that awaits us in heaven, Peter reminds us, is "imperishable, undefiled, and unfading" (1 Peter 1:4; compare Matt. 6:19–20). It is certainly ours now and cannot be taken from us—it is "kept . . . for [us]," and we "by God's power are being guarded through faith for a salvation ready to be revealed in the last time" (1 Peter 1:4–5). When Christ returns, we will fully take hold of this inheritance, and nothing will take away that joy from us!

Fourth, at best, the people in our lives are imperfectly sanctified (as are we!). When we leave this world, we enter into a sinless company: "innumerable angels in festal gathering," "the assembly of the firstborn who are enrolled in heaven, . . . the spirits of the righteous made perfect" (Heb. 12:22–23). It is not simply that we will be reunited with believing loved ones, but that our fellowship will be unlike any fellowship we have had on earth. We will be among angels and people who are sinlessly righteous (as we will be!).

Finally, to enter heaven is to enter the presence of "God, the judge of all," and "Jesus, the mediator of a new covenant" (Heb. 12:23–24). We will experience fellowship with the triune God more deeply and more richly than we have ever experienced on earth. David said, "As for me, I shall behold your face in righteousness; when I awake, I shall be satisfied with your likeness" (Ps. 17:15; compare Isa. 33:17; Rev. 22:3–4). To be fully satisfied with what alone can satisfy, the blessed presence of God—it is for this that we are exchanging a world that can never satisfy.

Conclusion

God transforms us through mind renewal (Rom. 12:2; Eph. 4:23). He wants us to think about this world (for what it is and isn't) and to think about heaven (for what it is and will be to us). This is one reason that God has showered us with tremendous helps—the gracious ministry of the Holy Spirit, the ministry of the Word of God, and the communion of the saints. Each of these gifts is designed to help us think well and walk confidently toward our heavenly home. What are you thinking about these days?

9

How Do I
Prepare for Death?
(Part 2)

We have begun to think about how to prepare ourselves for death. Preparing for death is the work of a lifetime. Central to this work are the spiritual disciplines we described in the previous chapter. But we need to do even more to ready ourselves and our loved ones for the hour of death. These preparations particularly involve our possessions and our bodies. We might think that these concerns are not addressed in the Bible, but this would be a mistake. God wants us to think biblically as we take up and act on these matters. If the concerns of chapter 8 fall especially under the first table of the law (the first four commandments), the concerns of this chapter fall especially under the second table of the law (the next six commandments). Preparing for death involves loving our neighbor as ourselves even as it involves loving the Lord our God with all our heart, soul, mind, and strength (see Mark 12:30–31).

In this chapter, we will think about preparing for death along four lines: How do we prepare our family and friends for our own death? How do we prepare our estate in anticipation of our death? How do we prepare ourselves and our family members to think through the end-of-life health questions that may meet us in the months and weeks before our death? How should we make preparations for our funeral and burial? In each of these areas, God has left us liberty. At the same time, He has not left us without direction in His

Word. We will turn to Scripture to look for those commands, principles, and examples that give us biblical answers to these questions.

Preparing Our Family and Friends

First, how do we prepare our family and friends when our death approaches? We may answer this question in two ways. The first way to prepare them is to share some final thoughts and reflections with them. Scripture reveals a long and rich biblical pattern of people who are nearing their deaths and are doing just that. In the Old Testament, Jacob gathers his sons and then blesses them with the promises that God had made to him, to Isaac, and to Abraham (Gen. 48:1–22). The book of Deuteronomy is an extended farewell speech from Moses to the people of Israel. Joshua gives a stirring exhortation at the close of his life and ministry (Josh. 24:1–28). David gives his son Solomon parting words of counsel and encouragement (1 Kings 2:1–9). In the New Testament, Jesus, on the eve of His death, speaks at length to His disciples to prepare them for what lay ahead of His crucifixion (see John 14–16). The Apostle Paul, convinced that he would never see them again, gives a farewell address to the Ephesian elders (Acts 20:17–38). Later, Paul, facing martyrdom in Rome, pens a farewell letter to Timothy (2 Timothy).

When we look at these words of farewell, we see certain themes and emphases common to them. We may look at three in particular. First, these addresses remind others of God's faithfulness. Specifically, they point them to all that God has done to save and to preserve His people, to His steadfast love and faithfulness. We see this concern driven home repeatedly in Moses' and Joshua's words of farewell. They remind Israel of all that God had done to bring His people out of Egypt, to preserve and provide for them in the wilderness, to bear patiently with them in their sins, and to bring them victoriously into the land. They say these things so that this new generation will be encouraged to trust and serve the Lord in the years ahead.

A second theme or emphasis is that God's people must put their trust in His promises. Jesus opens His Farewell Discourse by telling the disciples: "Let not your hearts be troubled. Believe in God; believe also in me" (John 14:1). Paul tells the Ephesian elders, "I commend you to God and to the word of his grace, which is able to build you up and to give you the inheritance among all those who are sanctified" (Acts 20:32). After rehearsing God's gracious purpose and saving work in Christ and his own call to preach the gospel, Paul tells Timothy, "I am not ashamed, for I know whom I have believed, and I am convinced that he is able to guard until that day what has been entrusted to me" (2 Tim. 1:12). It is as though Paul is saying to his younger colleague in ministry, "Timothy—I have trusted God, and He has never disappointed me. You can too!"

Third, these addresses call believers to a close walk with God. Joshua challenges the wilderness generation to "choose this day whom you will serve. . . . But as for me and my house, we will serve the LORD" (Josh. 24:15). Jesus tells His disciples, "If you love me, you will keep my commandments" (John 14:15). Paul calls Timothy to "share in suffering for the gospel by the power of God" (2 Tim. 1:8)—it is by suffering with and for the gospel that Timothy will enjoy fellowship with Christ (see Phil. 3:10). And it is, of course, by remembering who God is and by believing His promises given in Scripture that we may draw nearer to God and walk more closely with Him.

What each of these three strands shares with the others is its God-centeredness. Each, in different ways, calls others to look to God, to trust in God, and to keep near to God. In death, faith is concerned to point others not to itself but to its sole object, God in Christ Jesus.

We can share such thoughts and reflections with our family and friends in many ways. It can be done in a large gathering; it can be done one-on-one. It can be done at the last hour, but it can also be done well in advance. It can be done in person, or it can be done in writing. However we may choose to share our parting counsel with our loved ones, we stand in a long tradition of men who in the face of death pointed others to the living and true God (Jer. 10:10).

A second way to prepare our family and friends as our death draws near is to pursue reconciliation with any from whom we may be estranged. Is there anyone against whom we have sinned? (Has anyone sinned against us?) If so, and if there has been no attempt at reconciliation, we should take steps to do so. Jesus urges us to do this in life (and not just as death nears): "If you are offering your gift at the altar and there remember that your brother has something against you, leave your gift there before the altar and go. First be reconciled to your brother, and then come and offer your gift" (Matt. 5:23–24). Notice that Jesus expects *us* to take the initiative in reconciliation when a brother has something against us. We may not be able to control others' responses or reactions, but we have an obligation to approach them, in humility and in truth, to seek to be reconciled to them. Paul reminds us, "If possible, so far as it depends on you, live peaceably with all" (Rom. 12:18). If we have done all that is in our power to be reconciled to someone else, we have done what Christ wants from us. Our goal is to live—and die—as those whose words and lives point others to the God of peace.

Preparing Our Worldly Estate

When we leave this world, we leave behind all our possessions. Job reminds us, "Naked I came from my mother's womb, and naked shall I return" (Job 1:21). What will become of our possessions, goods, savings, and investments after we are gone? How may we best ensure that we have provided for our surviving spouse (or other family members)? These questions do not answer themselves. They require thoughtful and careful planning in advance of our death.

It is important to make these kinds of plans and preparations. If we die without having made any arrangements for our estate, then there can be serious consequences and repercussions. Our finances and property can be tied up in court, inaccessible to our surviving loved ones for a time. The unexpected and unwelcome discoveries that can come with a failure to plan well in advance can compound the grief and stress that our loved ones bear in the weeks and months after our death. Expenses—in taxes and fees—can be considerably higher if we have not made proper preparations in advance. And the lack of clarity or direction as to the disposal of our earthly goods and possessions can become the occasion for family division and strife.

For these reasons, we should (with our spouse) commit to crafting an appropriate, comprehensive, and legally acceptable plan to make sure that our possessions, accounts, and investments go where we want them to go. We should not wait until the last minute to make these decisions. They are important decisions. We need time to gather information and good counsel. This latter point is especially important. In crafting a plan, we should consult with financial and legal professionals who can help us make sure that we are making decisions that are both wise and in keeping with the law of the land.

In making these preparations, we are honoring the biblical command to love our neighbor as ourselves.[1] Paul tells Timothy that "if anyone does not provide for his relatives, and especially for members of his household, he has denied the faith and is worse than an unbeliever" (1 Tim. 5:8). To be sure, Paul is thinking about someone who is living and refuses to provide for his household, but the principle also applies to estate planning. We should do our very best to ensure that we have provided for our families, even and especially when we are no longer living. Doing so is a tangible demonstration of our Christianity.

As we make these plans, what sorts of concerns or priorities might we have in mind? We may raise two in particular. First, we should ask how we may provide for the needs of our family, particularly the spouse who survives us. Do we have children who are underage or who have special medical conditions? Do we have grandchildren whose circumstances would warrant our material support? Second, we should ask how we may contribute to the work and worship of the church, beyond our regular offerings. Are there kingdom-minded ministries and benevolences that we would like to support? In life, the believer provides for his family and contributes to the needs of the saints. Proper estate planning helps us continue our life's work even after we have finished our life's course. It is a way to demonstrate Christian love to those near and far for years to come.

Preparing for the End of Life

Some of the most difficult decisions that many people have to face are commonly called *end-of-life* decisions. We are blessed with wonderful medical technologies and treatments that can extend life beyond what was imaginable even a generation or two ago. But with these advances in medicine come some important and even agonizing decisions—decisions that often have to be made quickly and that have life-and-death implications.

As a starting point, we return to the law of God. The sixth commandment ("You shall not murder," Ex. 20:13) forbids us from the unjust taking of life, whether our own or someone else's. It requires us to make all lawful attempts to preserve our lives and others' lives.[2] We have a duty to preserve life, and God forbids us from taking life unjustly.

How does this obligation apply to the realm of end-of-life decisions?

It would require a book to address this question, much less answer it satisfactorily. Our aim is, in short scope, to prepare believers to answer those questions for the day when they may arise—whether for themselves or for their loved ones. We will offer some starting tips and then move to some working principles.

Starting Tips

The first tip is that while we are still in good mental and physical health, we should pick up and read good resources addressing end-of-life issues from a biblical point of view.[3] As we read them, we will get broad exposure to the medical questions and choices that we may face as we (or those we love) approach death. Since technologies and treatments are always changing, we should do our best to stay current with discussions of those developments.

Second, it is also important to seek out wise counselors whom we know and trust. Find a pastor or elder who can help you formulate a biblical approach to end-of-life issues. Consult trusted medical professionals who can help you with the medical dimensions of these questions and can bring to bear their experience in our current medical system. You could ask them such questions as these: "How do I practically and effectively work with my doctors? What sorts of things might they ask of me? What sorts of questions should I ask them? What should I do if I disagree with what my doctor recommends?"

Third, we should try to formulate our wishes, make them legal or official in whatever state we reside, and make them known to our family and medical professionals. One way to do this is through a living will. Another is by granting durable power of attorney for healthcare decisions to someone we love and trust. Living wills specify treatment options that we want and do not want if we become unable to make those decisions at the moment those treatment options are offered. Durable power of attorney legally empowers a loved one to make healthcare choices on our behalf when we are unable to do so. The decided benefit of this latter option is that it allows a loved one who knows us and our convictions to make nuanced decisions in light of often rapidly changing circumstances. It also means that we will have someone who will serve as our advocate when we are unable to communicate our wishes to medical professionals.[4]

Working Principles

While space prevents a comprehensive treatment of end-of-life issues, we may offer three broad working principles that will help us get a handle on some of the basic biblical guidelines involved in these questions and decisions.

The first is that unjust killing is always wrong. This principle derives directly from the sixth commandment ("You shall not murder," Ex. 20:13). Unjust killing occurs when we "take steps that intentionally end someone's life."[5] For this reason, what is commonly termed *euthanasia* is forbidden. We may not, for instance, administer to others or to ourselves medication that will cause death; nor may we ask a medical professional to administer such medication with this intention.

The second principle is to recognize that medicine, broadly speaking, seeks to bring a person from sickness to health.[6] This "larger goal of health" admits of what one Christian physician has recently identified as seven distinct and supporting goals of medicine—namely, to "cure, live longer, improve function, comfort, achieve a life goal, provide support for family, and clarify diagnosis or prognosis."[7] In many respects, the particular supporting goal of treatment is tied to the specific medical circumstances of a particular individual. For this reason, we should have conversations with our healthcare providers in which we candidly share with them our values and work with them to articulate goals that are both consistent with our values and appropriate to our present medical circumstances.[8] We should ask questions as these: "What is the purpose of this treatment?" "How likely is it that this treatment will accomplish that purpose?" "What are the costs associated with this treatment?" "Do the benefits that this treatment may impose on me outweigh the burdens?"[9] As we receive the ongoing counsel of our medical providers, measuring that advice against the teaching of Scripture, we will be best positioned to make informed and God-honoring decisions relating to our health.

The third principle recognizes that death is inevitable. No medical intervention can indefinitely prevent death, and no medical professional has the wisdom and skill to keep us alive forever. There will come a point when we must acknowledge that we are (or a loved one is) dying. When we realize that our body is dying, then we must change our approach to the medical care we are seeking. Some treatment options offered to us may extend life for a matter of weeks or months but will not change the inevitable outcome of death. We are under no biblical obligation to accept those treatment options. I may rather pursue a course of treatment that is not designed to cure me but is designed to make me comfortable as I approach the end of my days. Such palliative care is a way to help ensure that the remaining life of a person is lived in dignity and comfort.

Under certain circumstances, to refuse treatment or to withdraw treatment (such as a feeding tube or a ventilator) is not killing the patient, whether it is oneself or a loved one. If it is clear that such treatment is only prolonging the inevitable outcome of death and will not bring healing to the patient, then there is no medical justification for pursuing or continuing the treatment. There comes a point at which the body wants to die, and such efforts will not change that reality, only forestall it. But it is important to stress that such decisions, however difficult they may be, are in no way violations of the sixth commandment. "Letting die is not the same as killing."[10]

What exactly *are* we intending when we decide to refuse or withdraw such treatment? We are certainly not intending to kill. We are, rather, aiming to make the limited life that remains a good life. Fulfilling this aim may mean that a person's life will be shorter in duration, but it will not be rendered more miserable by interventions that cannot restore it to health.[11] "We should aim to live the right *kind* of life, not necessarily the *longest* life. Sometimes in fact the choice to live the right kind of life means that we cannot choose to live as long as possible."[12]

End-of-life decisions are difficult—intellectually, ethically, and emotionally. We should prepare ourselves in advance with biblical teaching to make these decisions in a way that honors God, following the commands that He has given us in the Bible. We should no less seek out godly spiritual and medical counsel (see Prov. 11:14; 15:22; 24:6). And above all, we should pray that God would bless these means to our good and to His glory.

Preparing for the Funeral and Burial

Finally, we should make appropriate preparations for our funeral and our burial. When it comes to the funeral, we should spare our grieving loved ones the burden of guessing (or second-guessing) what our wishes may have been. We should write out or clearly tell our loved ones the answers to questions such as the following: "What Scriptures do I want read at my funeral? What hymns or songs do I want sung? Which minister or ministers would I like to officiate? Where will the funeral be? Will there be pallbearers? Are there any military honors to be performed?"

We should also make advance arrangements for our burial. These arrangements can be emotionally depleting, time-consuming, and costly at the best of times. We should spare our loved ones the added burden of making these decisions in the short window of time between our death and our funeral.

One question that often arises in the church is whether Christians may choose to be cremated. Cremation has become more and more popular, not least because burial has become more and more expensive. To bury or to cremate can be a delicate and controversial question among some Christians.

The Bible does not allow us to make burial a matter of conscience. In other words, we may not say that it is a duty to bury and a sin to cremate. But while Scripture does not raise this question to the level of command and prohibition, it does express a preference for burial.[13] The typical practice of believers in both the Old Testament and the New Testament was to entomb the bodies of the deceased. This practice was carried over into church history, as Christians throughout the centuries have generally opted to bury their dead. Burying the dead conveys at least two important truths. First, it confirms the finality of death to those who observe the lowering of a loved one's remains into the ground. Second, it testifies to the hope of the resurrection. The believer's body is lowered into the ground in the confidence that at the last day, it will be raised in glory.

This latter point helps us appreciate a dimension of funerals and burials that can be easily missed. The funeral and the burial of a believer should bear witness to the gospel to all those who have gathered to mourn. Funerals and burials are one of those few occasions when unbelievers may find themselves under the ministry of the Word of God. What they need most is the comfort that only the gospel can bring to them.

It is worth all the time and energy that we invest to prepare for our funeral and burial. From beyond the grave, we are pointing our friends and family to the love of God in Jesus Christ. We are doing this because we love them. In fact, love to others is what prompts us to make preparations in the four areas we have considered in this chapter. Preparing our family and friends with final words of Christian counsel, preparing our worldly estate to support others after we have died, preparing to help ourselves and others live according to biblical principles at the end of life, and preparing our funeral and burial—each of these is motivated by love and is an expression of love in keeping with biblical principles. In showing love to those around us, we do so because God has first loved us (1 John 4:19). In showing love to those around us, we seek to point others to the love of God in Christ.

Part Three

BEYOND DEATH

10

What Does
the Bible Teach about
the Resurrection?

One of the joys of being a Christian is to know that in Jesus Christ there is eternal life beyond death. Jesus told Martha: "I am the resurrection and the life. Whoever believes in me, though he die, yet shall he live, and everyone who lives and believes in me shall never die" (John 11:25–26). By His death and resurrection, Jesus has delivered us from "the second death" and has brought us to eternal life (Rev. 20:14).

Having thought about what death is and how the believer should encounter death, we now take the time to think about the Bible's testimony to what lies beyond death—the bodily resurrection, the final judgment, and the eternal state (heaven and hell). We will begin by thinking about the resurrection from the dead. We saw in chapter 4 that believers have already begun to share in the resurrection life that Christ has won for us (Eph. 2:6; Col. 3:1). We share in that resurrection life fully only when our bodies are raised gloriously from the dead, forever reunited to our souls.

The whole Bible teaches the promise of the resurrection from the dead.[1] One place where Scripture specifically addresses the bodily resurrection in both extended and concentrated fashion is 1 Corinthians 15. We will follow the Apostle Paul as he shores up our faith in the resurrection, informs our understanding of the resurrection, and applies the resurrection to the lives of God's people.

Background to 1 Corinthians 15

What may we say about the concern that Paul addresses in this chapter? He is responding to false teaching in the Corinthian church. This false teaching was not being actively promoted by the whole church. Paul addresses "some of you" who "say that there is no resurrection of the dead" (1 Cor. 15:12). But even if only some of the congregation were advocating this view, Paul was concerned that this teaching would harm the whole church. That is why he addresses the whole church throughout this chapter ("brothers," vv. 1, 50, 58).

What did these individuals mean in denying the resurrection of the dead? It is doubtful that any in the church were outright denying the resurrection in the way that skeptics in our own day often do.[2] More likely, these persons believed in "life after death without a resurrection from the dead."[3] We know that Paul inhabited a world that responded to the doctrine of the bodily resurrection with scorn and derision (see Acts 17:32).[4] Ancients had no difficulty admitting that people lived as spirits beyond the grave. What they did not accept was that that life would be embodied.

For Paul, this is not an innocent error. Unlike the difference of opinion between the "strong" and the "weak" in the church in Rome (see Rom. 14:1–15:7), disagreement over the bodily resurrection from the dead carries consequences; the resurrection is not a nonessential doctrine on which believers may disagree in charity. For Paul, no Christian is at liberty to set aside the resurrection. It is essential to the biblical gospel.

For these reasons, Paul mounts an extended defense and exposition of the resurrection. His discussion in this chapter falls into four parts, each of which we may characterize by a single word that he uses in that section. In 1 Corinthians 15:1–11, Paul shows that the doctrine of the resurrection has been "delivered" to the church by the Apostles. It is therefore central and not peripheral to the Christian faith. In verses 12–34, Paul shows us "that" the resurrection must take place (v. 12).[5] In verses 35–49, Paul addresses the "how" of the resurrection (v. 35)—that is, how God will raise our bodies from the dead, and what those bodies will be like.[6] In verses 50–58, Paul helps us to see how the resurrection of Christ is "victory" to the believer (vv. 55–57). The resurrection gives us firm hope for the future and confidence to live for Christ in the present.

1 Corinthians 15:1–11: The Resurrection, "Delivered"

Paul first stresses that the resurrection is essential to the gospel. He reminds the Corinthians of what they already know—the gospel that he "preached" to them and that they "received" (1 Cor. 15:1). In this gospel they currently "stand" and are "being saved," as long as they "hold fast" to it (vv. 1–2). At no point in one's Christian experience—past, present, or future—can a Christian afford to let go of the gospel.

Since no Christian may ever let go of the *gospel*, Paul continues, it necessarily follows that no Christian may ever let go of the *resurrection*. This point becomes clear from his discussion of the gospel's contents in verses 3–4. The Apostle does not here remind the Corinthians of everything that he "delivered" to them but reminds them only of the matters "of first importance" (v. 3). At the heart of Paul's teaching is the gospel about Jesus Christ, who "died for our sins" and "was raised on the third day" (vv. 3–4). These two great facts—the death and resurrection of Christ—are attested facts. The fact of Jesus' death is demonstrated by His burial (v. 4). The fact of Jesus' resurrection is evidenced by His resurrection appearances to multiple people, including the Apostle Paul (vv. 5–8). The resurrection, then, is central to the gospel that Paul preached and that the Corinthians believed. It is an event of history, amply proved and deserving of full acceptance. It is impossible that one could extract the resurrection from the gospel and be left with a true and saving message of good news.

1 Corinthians 15:12–34: The "That" of the Resurrection

It is this point that launches the next section of Paul's argument: "Now if Christ is proclaimed as raised from the dead, how can some of you say that there is no resurrection of the dead?" (1 Cor. 15:12). Having established the resurrection as essential to the gospel message that one must believe for salvation, Paul now shows that the bodily resurrection of believers must take place. He does this by demonstrating the inseparability of the resurrection of Christ and the resurrection of the believer. Therefore, if the resurrection of Christ is necessary to the gospel message and to the salvation of the believer, no less is the bodily resurrection necessary to the gospel and to one's salvation.

Paul demonstrates this point in an intriguing way. He argues that if you deny *our* resurrection, you necessarily deny *Christ's* resurrection.

If there is no resurrection of the dead, then not even Christ has been raised. (v. 13)

[God] did not raise [Christ] if it is true that the dead are not raised. (v. 15)

For if the dead are not raised, not even Christ has been raised. (v. 16)

Why is this the case? Why does *Christ's* resurrection stand or fall on *our* bodily resurrection? The answer lies in the union between Christ and the believer. Paul tells us that "as in Adam all die, so also in Christ shall all be made alive" (v. 22). To strike at the resurrection of the one is necessarily to strike at the resurrection of the other.

Paul helps us understand this relationship in the verses surrounding verse 22. "Christ has been raised from the dead, the *firstfruits* of those who have fallen asleep" (v. 20, emphasis added). "But each in his own order: Christ the *first-fruits*, then at his coming those who belong to Christ" (v. 23, emphasis added). When Paul says that Christ is the "firstfruits," he is drawing an image from the world of agriculture.[7] To be sure, Paul is asserting that Christ's resurrection comes before our own. He was, after all, raised from the dead two thousand years ago, and we still await the bodily resurrection. But that is not all that he is saying. Just as the firstfruits is the first installment of a single, larger harvest, so Christ's resurrection is the first installment of one great "resurrection" harvest.

Seen from that light, we can understand why Paul insists that to deny our resurrection is to deny Christ's resurrection. To deny that there is a harvest necessarily denies the existence of the firstfruits. Our resurrection and Christ's resurrection are so bound up together that the one requires the other. Because Christ has been raised from the dead, it necessarily follows that we will be raised from the dead. If one denies our resurrection, then one has necessarily denied Christ's resurrection.

In verses 12–19, Paul hypothetically entertains the proposition that "there is no resurrection of the dead" (v. 13). This would mean that "not even Christ has been raised" (v. 13). What are the implications of saying that Christ was not raised from the dead? In the first place, the Apostles' "preaching is in vain" (v. 14), and our "faith is in vain" or "futile" (vv. 14, 17). Second, the Apostles are "misrepresenting God" by telling people that God raised Jesus from the dead when, in fact, He did no such thing (v. 15). Third, we "are still in [our] sins" (v. 17). Christ was "raised for our justification" (Rom. 4:25), and if Christ was not raised, then we are still under condemnation.[8] Moreover, "those also who have fallen asleep in Christ have perished" (1 Cor. 15:18)—they have died in their sins, condemned and without hope of mercy from God. Finally, for those of us who are still alive, "if in Christ we have hope in this life only, we are of all people most to be pitied" (v. 19). We are truly pathetic, since our only hope and confidence would have no basis in fact.

Mercifully, that is not the case: "But in fact Christ has been raised from the dead" (v. 20). What are the implications of the fact of Christ's resurrection (and ours to come)? In verses 24–28, Paul directs our attention to the certain victory guaranteed by Christ's resurrection. The risen Christ now reigns (v. 25). His enemies are currently being subjugated to Him (v. 27). When the "end" comes—the day when Christ returns in glory to bring history to its conclusion and to judge the world in righteousness—then "all his enemies" will be "under his feet," including "death" (vv. 24, 25, 27, 26). The "kingdom," now complete and full, will be handed to the Father (v. 24), and, of course, we will be raised from the dead (v. 23).

Paul concludes this section by drawing implications from Christ's resurrection victory for the Christian life in the here and now (vv. 29–34).[9] In particular, Paul highlights the stresses and dangers of Christian living and service. "We [are] in danger every hour," Paul states, and "I die every day!" (vv. 30–31). "If the dead are not raised," then what "gain" comes to him for his enduring persecutions in Ephesus (v. 32)? Only if the resurrection is true do sufferings and losses for Christ have any meaning at all. Otherwise, Paul concludes, "let us eat and drink, for tomorrow we die" (v. 32). Denying the resurrection cuts the nerve of Christian endeavor and perseverance. The Corinthians must put off this false teaching right away before it corrodes and corrupts the church even further (vv. 33–34).

The resurrection, Paul argues in this second section of the chapter, is absolutely necessary. To deny our bodily resurrection is to deny Christ's resurrection. If Christ has not been raised, then our faith is empty, our hope is vain, and our sufferings as believers are meaningless. The only thing one can do is live a life of sinful self-indulgence before death snuffs out all opportunity for pleasure. But, Paul declares, Christ has been raised from the dead. We have a sure hope for the future and motivation and power to do hard things for Christ in the present. The Corinthians must put an end to this false teaching right away.

1 Corinthians 15:35–49: The "How" of the Resurrection

Paul next quotes someone asking a question: "How are the dead raised? With what kind of body do they come?" (1 Cor. 15:35). He immediately rebukes the inquirer: "You foolish person!" (v. 36). Since Paul goes on to answer this question, he must not think that it is an entirely foolish one to ask. Likely Paul is rebuking the skepticism lurking behind it. In the mind of the one asking this question, the bodily resurrection is foolish and irrational: "How can a dead and decayed body come to life? What kind of body would that be, anyway?"

Paul takes this "Gotcha!" question and offers a rational answer. He patiently replies to the objector's belief that it is impossible for the dead to come to life (vv. 35–41). He then positively explains what the resurrection body will be like (vv. 42–49).

In the first place, Paul demonstrates that the doctrine of the resurrection is not irrational. After all, he reasons, God has liberally scattered helps throughout creation to understand the resurrection. When you plant a seed, "a bare kernel," what goes into the ground "is not the body that is to be" (v. 37). Since "what you sow does not come to life unless it dies," the result of planting a seed is analogous to the resurrection (v. 36). The living plant that appears has emerged from the seed, but there has been a profound change. What we now see is the "body" that "God . . . has chosen" and "give[n]" (v. 38). "The self-same seed that 'dies' in the ground is 'raised' in a transformed 'body.'"[10] In a similar way, God will raise our bodies from the dead.

Paul then observes that there are different kinds of "flesh" in the creation—"one kind for humans, another for animals, another for birds, and another for fish. There are heavenly bodies and earthly bodies" (vv. 39–40a). If God has set a diversity of bodies in the creation now, why is it impossible to conceive that our present bodies will be transformed at the resurrection? Furthermore, if there is "glory" that belongs to "heavenly" bodies, distinct from the "kind" of glory that now belongs to earthly bodies, why can't a similar diversity of glory characterize our resurrection bodies in comparison with our present bodies (vv. 40b–41; compare vv. 47–48)?

In the second place, having shown that the resurrection is not at all irrational, Paul proceeds to describe what our resurrection bodies will be like (1 Cor. 15:42–49). He does so by comparing our resurrection bodies with our preresurrection bodies in four ways. First, our bodies now are "perishable," but then they will be "imperishable" (v. 42). Currently, our bodies are susceptible to disease, injury, decay, and ultimately death. But in the resurrection, they will be free from all those things. Second, our bodies are now marked by "dishonor," but then they will be marked by "glory" (v. 43a). Our first parents were created without shame (see Gen. 2:25). Only because of sin did shame and dishonor enter the human experience (see 3:7). Because of sin, people fall short of the glory of God (Rom. 3:23). But our resurrected bodies, entirely free from sin and misery, will be glorious, just as the resurrection body of Jesus Christ is glorious (Phil. 3:21). Third, our bodies exist in "weakness" now, but they will be "raised in power" (1 Cor. 15:43). Weakness characterizes existence in this present age (2 Cor. 12:9), and when Christ died on the cross, He died in "weakness" (13:4). But Christ now "lives by the power of God" (13:4). Our resurrection bodies will also participate in this power—the power of God that characterizes the age to come.

Fourth, our bodies are currently "natural," but our resurrection bodies will be "spiritual" (1 Cor. 15:44a). We should not misunderstand Paul here. He is not saying that our resurrection bodies will be beyond the reach of the senses. Jesus' resurrection body, after all, is a living, breathing *body*. He told His disciples: "Touch me, and see. For a spirit does not have flesh and bones as you see that I have" (Luke 24:39). He even "took" and "ate" a "piece of broiled fish" in the presence of His disciples (24:43, 42). The risen Jesus is no ghost, and neither will we be in the resurrection.

What, then, is the contrast between our present "natural" bodies and our "spiritual" resurrection bodies? In the remainder of this section, Paul shows us that the "natural" body is the one that belonged to Adam at the creation (1 Cor. 15:44b–45a). The "spiritual" body is the resurrection body of Christ. Paul terms it "spiritual" because Jesus was raised in the power of the Holy Spirit (v. 45b). He is so possessed by the Holy Spirit that His body is "spiritual"—that is, "brought forth and determined by the divine, heavenly power."[11] Our bodies, no less, will be "spiritual." We will "bear the image of the man of heaven" (v. 49)—that is to say, we will be fully conformed to the Lord Jesus Christ in every way that a redeemed sinner can be.

How, then, may we summarize Paul's description of the resurrection body? In the first place, Paul is insistent that it will be *our* body. We will not exchange our present body for one that is completely different. Rather, our present body will be completely and thoroughly transformed. In the second place, Christ's resurrection body is the template for our own. The descriptors of our future resurrection body in 1 Corinthians 15:42–45 are descriptors of Christ's present resurrection body. As our present body is patterned and defined by the "first man," so our resurrection body will be patterned and defined by the "second man" (v. 47).

In this chapter, Paul has been addressing the resurrection of believers. That raises the question, Will the wicked be raised? The answer of Scripture is yes. We read in Daniel 12:2 that "many of those who sleep in the dust of the earth shall awake, some to everlasting life, and some to shame and everlasting contempt." Jesus speaks of both the "resurrection of life" and the "resurrection of judgment" (John 5:29). Speaking to Felix, Paul declared that there would "be a resurrection of both the just and the unjust" (Acts 24:15). All people will be raised from the dead when Jesus Christ returns in glory.

The Bible does not reflect at great length on the resurrection bodies of the wicked, but we may make a couple of observations. First, the wicked will be raised bodily because they sinned in the body. Thus, they must be judged, condemned, and punished in the body. Second, whereas the resurrection bodies of believers will be glorious and honorable, the resurrection bodies of the wicked will be characterized by disgrace and dishonor (Dan. 12:2). As condemned sinners, they will spend eternity in shame and under the judgment of God. Their bodies will be suited to this condition.

The future resurrection of all people impresses on us the urgency of the gospel. Because of sin, we deserve eternal death. Those who die outside Jesus Christ will ultimately experience this death in their whole person, soul and body. But in Jesus Christ alone there is hope of eternal life. And this hope is for the whole person, soul and body. In the closing verses of this chapter, Paul helps us rejoice in this hope and to draw encouragement from it for our present lives.

1 Corinthians 15:50–58: The "Victory" of the Resurrection

Paul brings his argument to a stirring, even poetic, conclusion. He reminds us that the resurrection is a "mystery" (1 Cor. 15:51). He does not mean that we should think of the resurrection like an Agatha Christie whodunit. The word "mystery" is a technical term in the New Testament, referring to something that God has revealed. The resurrection is just such a revelation. When Christ returns—"at the last trumpet"—"the dead will be raised imperishable, and we shall be changed" (v. 52).[12]

Christ's return and our resurrection from the dead will bring to fulfill-ment the words of Isaiah 25:8 and Hosea 13:14: "'Death is swallowed up in victory.' 'O death, where is your victory? O death, where is your sting?'" (1 Cor. 15:54b–55). That is to say, the resurrection of the dead will mark the complete conquest of death. Paul explains why this is so: "The sting of death is sin, and the power of sin is the law" (v. 56). In His death and resurrection, Christ paid for and set us free from the penalty that the law exacts for sin. Since "sin" is the "sting of death," Christ has removed death's sting for us. We will fully and finally share in Christ's victory over death when our bodies are gloriously raised from the dead. Christ has already accomplished this victory in His death and resurrection. We began to share in His victory the moment we came to faith in Christ and were justified in Christ (see v. 57). And we will fully share in His victory when we are raised bodily from the dead. With death's sting removed, all that remains is for death to be "swallowed up"!

While Christ's past victory gives us certain hope for the future, it also reaches into our present: "Therefore, my beloved brothers, be steadfast, immovable, always abounding in the work of the Lord, knowing that in the Lord your labor is not in vain" (v. 58). Paul knows that we might be asking ourselves, "If death brings an end to all my work and labors in this age, then what is the point of devoting my time and energies to them?" The answer to that question lies in the hope of the resurrection that Paul has spent fif-ty-seven verses explaining ("Therefore . . . ," v. 58). The resurrection gives our work meaning in the here and now: "In the Lord your labor is not in vain." Because Christ has been raised from the dead, and because we will also be raised, our this-worldly endeavors have eternal significance in Jesus Christ. Paul has told us that our faith is not "in vain" because Christ has been raised from the dead (v. 14). The grace of God toward Paul was not "in vain," as demonstrated by Paul's faithful, grace-enabled Apostolic labors (v. 10). And now, he tells us, "in the Lord," our "labor is not in vain" (v. 58).[13] The resurrection prevents our day-to-day lives from being consigned to vanity. Whether it is trusting in Jesus Christ or serving Christ in the full range of the callings that He assigns to each one of us, the resurrection ensures that our endeavors in this world, done for Jesus Christ ("the work of the Lord," v. 58), have meaning. Christ takes note of them and will be pleased to graciously reward them when we appear before Him.

For this reason, Paul declares, we should "be steadfast, immovable, always abounding in the work of the Lord" (v. 58). Because the resurrection gives significance to all kinds of service done in faith and love to Jesus Christ, we should be both firm and fruitful in that service. To lose sight of the resurrection has palpable consequences for the way we go about our jobs, for our relationships with our family and friends, and for our service within the church. If we are to serve Christ well in all of life, we need a clear-eyed view of the resurrection.

Conclusion

Paul is adamant—the resurrection is an essential element of the gospel. Without the resurrection, we have no gospel, no faith, and no hope. Without the resurrection, our suffering and trials (1 Cor. 15:30–31) and our "labor" (v. 58) have no meaning whatsoever. Paul does not worry that we think about the resurrection too much. He wants us to think about the resurrection more than we do. This is because the resurrection is part of our inheritance and heritage as believers in Christ and because the resurrection gives meaning to the trials and drudgery that lie before us day after day. Do you make it a point to think about the resurrection of Christ and of your own bodily resurrection to come?

The hope of the resurrection is a hope for the body. We often think of salvation in terms of our souls, and that is true as far as it goes. But salvation no less concerns the body. We will not shed our bodies the way that snakes shed their skins. Our bodies will be resurrected and forever reunited to our souls. Christ has saved not part of me but all of me.

This truth gives us hope as we witness our bodies breaking down under the wear and tear of physical life in a fallen world, and ultimately in the approach of death. This decay is only temporary. "In a moment, in the twinkling of an eye, at the last trumpet," our bodies will be raised, imperishable and immortal (vv. 52, 54). Therefore, we can bear the dissolution of our bodies in faith and patience because we know the glorious future that has been promised to us.

This truth also calls us to live holy lives in the here and now. Paul earlier reminded the Corinthians that they "were bought with a price. So glorify God in your body" (6:20). Our bodies are precious because Christ bought them with His own blood. We will inhabit our bodies forever, and they have a glorious destiny. Our bodies are prized in God's sight. We should not neglect our bodies but care for them. We should not allow our bodies to participate in sin but should "present [ourselves] to God as those who have been brought from death to life" (Rom. 6:13a). How does the way that you treat and use your body reflect the truth of the resurrection?

11

What Does the Bible Teach about the Final Judgment?

The Bible teaches frequently and emphatically that final judgment awaits us. To be sure, immediately after people die, they go before God, who then casts the souls of the impenitent into hell and brings the souls of His people into His favorable presence. Yet there remains a final judgment for all human beings. This will take place after the resurrection, when soul and body will have been forever reunited. Furthermore, this judgment will be "public," in the presence of angels and the whole human race.[1]

In this chapter, we are going to think about the Bible's teaching about the final judgment along four lines. First, we will see that the final judgment is a doctrine that is essential to the biblical gospel. Second, we will ask and answer some basic questions about the final judgment. Third, we will think about what both the righteous and the wicked will undergo at the final judgment. Finally, we will explore why Christians must face the final judgment but why we should not fear it.

The Final Judgment—a Gospel Essential

It might seem strange at first to hear someone say that the final judgment is essential to the biblical gospel. After all, how does the looming reality of divine judgment fit into the "good news" that the gospel brings to sinners? We may answer that question along two related lines. First, Paul tells us that it was essential to his gospel proclamation. In Romans 2:12–16, the Apostle discusses the accountability to God of gentiles who do not have the written law of God. He speaks of "that day when, *according to my gospel*, God judges the secrets of men by Christ Jesus" (2:16, emphasis added). The final judgment is a part of the gospel message that Paul preached. We see examples of this in Paul's preaching in Acts. He tells the Athenians gathered at the Areopagus that God "has fixed a day on which he will judge the world in righteousness by a man whom he has appointed; and of this he has given assurance to all by raising him from the dead" (Acts 17:31).[2] When he was granted an audience before the Roman governor Felix, Paul "reasoned about righteousness and self-control and the coming judgment" (Acts 24:25).

Why was Paul committed to declaring the final judgment as part of his gospel proclamation? The final judgment is, of course, bad news to a sinner unreconciled to God. The knowledge of it should impress on such persons their plight and their helplessness to extract themselves from it. The knowledge of the final judgment should awaken people to seek for some relief. What makes the gospel "good news" is precisely the relief that it offers—the mercy of God in and through the death and resurrection of Jesus Christ.

Second, the final judgment helps us understand the work of Christ on sinners' behalf. The New Testament is insistent that what Christ endured at the cross was the judgment of God. He died accursed and forsaken of God, not for any wrong that He had committed but because He was the righteous and willing sin bearer for His people.[3] He paid the penalty that was due to us for our sins: "Christ redeemed us from the curse of the law by becoming a curse for us—for it is written, 'Cursed is everyone who is hanged on a tree'" (Gal. 3:13). Therefore, the moment that a person believes in Jesus Christ, he knows that Christ has made on his behalf full satisfaction to the justice of God. In Christ, we will not stand condemned at the final judgment because Christ has already been condemned in our place. In fact, far from being condemned, we are now declared righteous in Jesus Christ (Rom. 8:1, 33–34). The sole basis of this verdict of justification is the righteousness of Christ, imputed to the sinner and received through faith alone. This righteousness, we have seen, consists of the full satisfaction and the perfect obedience of Christ. Jesus has fully answered the law's demands for righteousness on our behalf. This righteousness, and the verdict that this righteousness carries with it, is our possession right now, through faith in Christ. We therefore already know in the present what the outcome of the final judgment will be—"justified"!

To remove or diminish the place of the final judgment in the biblical gospel therefore necessarily removes or diminishes what Christ accomplished on the cross.[4] The gospel confronts sinners with the stark and unavoidable reality of the final judgment at the end of history. It gloriously declares that Jesus Christ underwent divine judgment on the cross and that everyone who trusts in Him can know that all his obligations as a sinner before the throne of final judgment have been met by Jesus Christ. In fact, every believer will stand—then as now—vindicated before God, robed in the imputed righteousness of Christ. The gospel tells us: "You must all undergo final judgment. Will you face it in Christ, the refuge of sinners, or will you dare to face it yourself?"

Basic Questions about the Final Judgment

Now that we have seen the importance of the final judgment to the biblical gospel, we may pose to Scripture some questions about the judgment. First, *Whom?* Whom will God gather for this final judgment? The Bible tells us that the wicked angels will stand before God then: "The angels who did not stay within their own position of authority, but left their proper dwelling, he has kept in eternal chains under gloomy darkness until the judgment of the great day" (Jude 6; compare 1 Cor. 6:3).[5] The Bible also tells us that all human beings will be brought before God in judgment. This gathering will include "all the nations" (Matt. 25:32), both those who are living and those who have died (Rev. 20:11–15).[6] And the final judgment will include believers, as Paul reminds us: "For we must all appear before the judgment seat of Christ, so that each one may receive what is due for what he has done in the body, whether good or evil" (2 Cor. 5:10).

Second, *When?* When will the final judgment occur? We may answer this in two ways. First, this judgment will occur immediately after the resurrection of the dead. Jesus tells us that "an hour is coming when all who are in the tombs will hear his voice and come out, those who have done good to the resurrection of life, and those who have done evil to the resurrection of judgment" (John 5:28–29). So then, when Christ returns, all the dead will be raised, and all people will be brought immediately into judgment before God. Second, we do not know the moment of time when Christ will return (Matt.

24:36). The time of His return has been fixed by the Father, but the Father has not seen fit to reveal it to us. Since the resurrection and the last judgment immediately follow the return of Christ, we do not know the precise time of these events either.

Third, *Who?* Who will render judgment on the last day? The New Testament tells us that the Father has entrusted "all judgment to the Son" (John 5:22). What may we say about Christ the Judge? First, the One who will judge us is God. He is our Maker, our Sustainer, and also our Judge. He is omniscient; nothing will escape His notice. He is impartial; His verdicts will be fair and without bias. He is righteous; there will be nothing unjust or unrighteous about His judgments. Second, the One who will judge us is a human being (Acts 17:31). He has the same nature that we do. He has firsthand acquaintance with what it means to live as a human being in a fallen world. Third, the One who will judge us is the Prophet, Priest, and King of His church. Those who have rejected Him will have to stand before Him to give an account of that rejection (as well as all their other sins). Those who belong to Him have the "unspeakable comfort" of knowing that their Judge is the One they call Savior and Friend.[7]

Fourth, *How?* With what standard will God judge us? The answer, in brief, is the law of God. Everyone, in at least one of two ways, has access to and knowledge of God's law. Paul tells us in Romans 2:12–16 that "the work of the law is written" on the "hearts" of unbelieving gentiles, their consciences testifying to their duty before God (Rom. 2:15). This awareness explains why these gentiles "by nature do what the law requires" (v. 14). It also explains their culpability before God. Even though gentiles "do not have the law" (v. 14)— that is, the written law that God gave to Israel— they are accountable to Him for transgressing its moral demands (see 1:18–32). Their consciences inform them of these demands and accuse them for breaking or failing to keep God's righteous standards.

All human beings receive this testimony. Some human beings also know the law of God in written form. This was true of the Jews under the Old Testament (and remains so today), and it is true of the Christian church in the present day. This outward benefit is an "advantage," Paul says, but it also carries with it greater responsibility (Rom. 3:1). As Jesus teaches, "Everyone to whom much was given, of him much will be required, and from him to whom they entrusted much, they will demand the more" (Luke 12:48). Greater light carries greater responsibility. But in every case, since all human beings have the law, God's judgment is just. One will be held to account according to the measure of what God has revealed to him.

Fifth, *What?* What will take place at the final judgment? The Son of God will send His angels to gather the elect (Matt. 24:31). He will gather angels and all human beings before Him (v. 31). In that great public assembly, He will then pronounce sentence on each one. That sentence will then be carried out. Christ will usher the elect into heaven. The elect angels who have gathered the elect to God for this judgment (v. 31) will usher the wicked to eternal punishment (13:41–42, 49–50).

The Wicked, the Righteous, and the Final Judgment

We may now briefly think about the distinct experiences of the wicked and the righteous on that day.[8] What will happen to the wicked? Having been resurrected in shame and dishonor, they will be brought before their Judge. They will stand before Christ as His unreconciled enemies. Jesus will pronounce sentence and provide evidence for that sentence (see Matt. 25:42–43). As we have already seen, He will judge each person according to the standard of revelation given to him. Judgment will also be proportionate to one's sins (10:15; 11:22, 24). This is because some sins are more heinous than others (John 19:11) and because certain conditions and circumstances render some sins more heinous than they would otherwise have been.[9]

When judgment is pronounced, the wicked will acknowledge the justice of their sentence. Their own consciences will concur with God's verdict, and their mouths will be stopped (see Rom. 2:15–16; 3:19). Because the sentence is just, in accordance with the truth, and final, there will be no appeal from it.

What about those who are in Christ Jesus? What will happen to the righteous on that day? Having dispatched His angels to gather the elect, Jesus will set the elect on His right hand (Matt. 24:31; 25:33). He will then "say to those on his right, 'Come, you who are blessed by my Father, inherit the kingdom prepared for you from the foundation of the world'" (25:34; compare 10:32). Each of the righteous, in company with all other human beings, will "give an account of himself to God" (Rom. 14:12). Paul tells the Corinthians, "We must all appear before the judgment seat of Christ, so that each one may receive what is due for what he has done in the body, whether good or evil" (2 Cor. 5:10).

This final account before Christ is not the justification of the Christian on the basis of the life that he has lived. On the contrary, every believer appears before Christ as one who has already been justified solely on the basis of the righteousness of Christ imputed to him, received through faith alone. The final verdict, we have seen, was rendered at the moment of the person's justification. Nothing that happens at the final judgment can overturn or modify that verdict.

Why Christians Must Face the Final Judgment but Not Fear It

For what purpose, then, must believers give an account of their lives to Jesus Christ at the final judgment? This question inevitably raises an additional question. Is the final judgment something that should provoke anxiety and dread in a believer's heart? We will see from Scripture why the believer must face the final judgment but should not fear it.

Facing the Final Judgment

There are at least five reasons that believers must face the final judgment. The first concerns the justice of God. God is a just Judge and therefore judges without partiality (Rom. 2:11; compare 1 Peter 1:17). God cannot show preferential treatment to Christians by exempting them from the evaluation that the rest of human beings will have to undergo. In justice He brings all human beings—Christians and non-Christians—before the bar of judgment.

Second, at the judgment, God will put on display public evidence of the work of grace in our lives. As our good works serve to demonstrate the truth of our faith in this life (see James 2:14–26), so they will display on an even grander scale the saving work of God in us (see Matt. 25:35–36). Furthermore, Peter tells us that just as our good works currently "put to silence the ignorance of foolish people" (1 Peter 2:15), so the sight of our "good deeds" will prompt those who slander us now to "glorify God on the day of visitation" (v. 12). In more than one way, then, the display of the good works of the elect at the final judgment will redound to the glory of God.

Third, the knowledge that we will one day stand before God in future judgment provides encouragement and direction to our lives in the present.

It guides our walk in the present in the fear of the Lord and in fellowship with Christ.[10] Knowing that we will give an account for what we think, say, and do should keep us from entertaining temptation and from committing sin. Jesus warns us, "Watch yourselves lest your hearts be weighed down with dissipation and drunkenness and cares of this life, and that day come upon you suddenly like a trap" (Luke 21:34). The coming judgment should encourage us to serve God faithfully and zealously in the pursuit of holiness. Peter tells us: "Since all these things are thus to be dissolved, what sort of people ought you to be in lives of holiness and godliness[?] . . . Therefore, beloved, since you are waiting for [new heavens and a new earth in which righteousness dwells], be diligent to be found by him without spot or blemish, and at peace" (2 Peter 3:11, 14). This judgment should also provide consolation as we undergo trials and face resistance for our faithful service to Christ, as Paul reminds the Thessalonians in 2 Thessalonians 1:5–10. Therefore, knowing that Christ is returning to judge the world should prompt us to "stay awake" and "be ready" (Matt. 24:42, 44).

Fourth, at the judgment, God will reconcile believers who remained unreconciled to one another at death. It is a sad reality of life in the church that divisions—sometimes sharp divisions—break out between Christians in the church. When that happens, each party should pray for and pursue reconciliation with the other. Sometimes they are reconciled. But sometimes they are not. Attempts at reconciliation may prove unsuccessful. Death may prevent further attempts. At the judgment, God will require an account of every believer. One of the blessed fruits of this accounting is that any remaining breaches among believers will be forever removed. Whatever may have divided them in life will prove no barrier to their blessed and uninterrupted fellowship in heaven.

Fifth, the final judgment will be the occasion at which God dispenses rewards to His people. The thought of rewards may unnerve some Christians—"Doesn't this compromise the Bible's teaching that salvation is by grace alone?" It should not, since rewards are a clear and consistent teaching of Scripture (see, for instance, Luke 6:35; 1 Cor. 3:10–15; 2 Tim. 4:8). So they are no threat to or contradiction of the Bible's teaching that salvation is by the grace of God alone. How, then, are we to think about the rewards granted at the final judgment?

In the first place, we should recognize that every Christian is justified on the same basis—the imputed righteousness of Christ alone. Every believer has a title to heaven on one ground and one ground only, "the free gift of righteousness" (Rom. 5:17). No believer, then, is admitted into heaven or excluded from it on the basis of anything that he has done.

Furthermore, when the Bible speaks of rewards, it often emphasizes the differences of rewards among Christians. Jesus makes this point in His parable of the minas (Luke 19:11–27). The master distributes minas to his servants, one mina for each servant. Each servant earns a different sum with that mina and is rewarded proportionately—the servant who earns ten minas is awarded ten cities; the servant who earns five minas is awarded five cities. There is therefore evident disparity of rewards among the elect in heaven.

How should we think of these two strands of biblical teaching—that every believer is admitted into heaven on exactly the same basis and that there are differences of rewards among those believers? We should first stress that no believer merits his reward from God. Even if we were to do the whole of our duty flawlessly, we would be "unworthy servants" (Luke 17:10). None of us ever deserves anything from God. The rewards, then, are rewards only of grace. "When God rewards the righteous for their good works, he only adds grace to grace, rewarding believers for those deeds which he himself works in them by his Spirit (John 15:1–17)."[11] The rewards have been merited—but not by us. "The essential merit that earned [them] is Christ's."[12]

If the rewards are rewards of grace, how may we think about the disparity of rewards among believers? The "reward is 'according to,' but not 'on account of' the works."[13] Our good works are never the basis of God's reward to us, but they are the measure according to which God dispenses His rewards. What, then, are these rewards? Rewards have to do with the measure of one's spiritual delight in God in heaven. Every resident of heaven will be "perfectly happy, but yet each one according to his own degree."[14] Jonathan Edwards observed: "For all shall be perfectly happy, every one shall be perfectly satisfied. Every vessel that is cast into this ocean of happiness is full, though there are some vessels far larger than others."[15] Every vessel is filled full, but some vessels are able to contain more than others. The rewards of grace, then, are the increased capacity for joy and satisfaction in heaven. God offers these rewards to us in order to encourage us to pursue holiness in this life. The greater the advances we make in holiness and service to God in this life, the greater the degree of happiness we will enjoy in the next life.[16]

Not Fearing the Final Judgment

Christians will face the final judgment, but they should not face it with anxiety or dread. Certainly, the Apostle Paul did not. He longed for the Lord to return quickly (1 Cor. 16:22). Every believer, Paul tells us, "love[s] his appearing" (2 Tim. 4:8). Why may we face the final judgment with reverent confidence, expectation, and joy?

First, to return to a point that we have raised more than once, every believer will come to the final judgment having already been justified. We are justified the moment that we believe. That verdict is final and unchangeable. In Christ, we will be no more justified on that day than we are right now. There is therefore no uncertainty as to the outcome of the final judgment.

Second, the One who will judge us is the One who has saved us and now intercedes for us. When Christ returns, He "will then come as [believers'] Redeemer and Savior, not to reproach them for their sins, but to fulfill his promises in them and to manifest the wonders of his grace."[17] For this reason, Jesus exhorts us, "straighten up and raise your heads, because your redemption is drawing near" (Luke 21:28). At His appearing, He is completing His work of grace in our lives. The last thing that we would expect Jesus to do is to reject us or cast us away. Furthermore, when Christ renders judgment on our lives, He is evaluating His own work in us. He will take great delight in beholding the fruit of His grace in our lives. That, in turn, should encourage us to look forward to that day and to prepare for it by living now for the glory of Christ.

Third, what about our sins? The Bible says that we will have to give an account to God for them (2 Cor. 5:10). Does this mean that my sins—even my secret sins—will be publicly placarded before the watching world at the last day? Will that day be to my overwhelming shame and horror? The Bible indicates that the answer to both these questions is no.[18] For one thing, our God is a God of mercy. He has pardoned our sins, covering them with the blood of His beloved Son. In doing so, He tells us, He has "cast all our sins into the depths of the sea" (Mic. 7:19) and He has "cast all [our] sins behind [His] back" (Isa. 38:17). Given these promises, we would not expect the final judgment to be an occasion when God casts those sins back into our faces.[19]

Further, the return of Christ will not be an occasion of shame and dishonor for God's people. It will be the occasion of the glory of Christ in His people.[20]

Every Christian will undergo final judgment at the return of Christ. We should not be indifferent to or cavalier about this judgment, but neither should we be craven and paralyzed with terror. It is a solemn thing to give an account of oneself and one's life to one's Maker and Judge. But when we remember that we approach the throne of God as persons already justified, that the Judge who sits on the throne is our Savior who once hung on the cross, who in love poured out His own blood to cover all our sins, even the deepest and vilest ones, and that this meeting will be glorious and delightful to Jesus, we can think about the final judgment in the way that God wants us to think about it. Let us anticipate that day with joy, and let us pursue heavenly joys by striving now for the "holiness without which no one will see the Lord" (Heb. 12:14).

12

What Does the Bible Teach about Heaven and Hell?

The crowning events of human history are the resurrection of the dead and the final judgment. At that point, all angels and human beings are ushered into one of two eternal states: heaven or hell. What does the Bible teach about heaven and hell? We also need to ask why the Bible reveals what it does about them. In other words, for what purposes has God spoken to us, in the middle of history, about realities that lie beyond the end of history? These two questions—"What?" and "Why?"—will guide our survey of what the Bible says about heaven and hell.

What Does the Bible Teach about Heaven?

An Embodied State

The Bible tells us at least five things about heaven. First, heaven will be an embodied state. That is to say, we will be in heaven, soul *and* body. In heaven, our souls will have been perfected in holiness. But our bodies will also have been raised from the dead and reunited to our souls. Because death has been "swallowed up in victory," our souls and bodies will never again be separated (1 Cor. 15:54). We will experience heaven in our imperishable, glorious, and spiritual resurrection bodies (vv. 42–43).

For this reason, this embodied experience of heaven will be a decided improvement over our experience of heaven in the intermediate state—that is, the state of believers between their deaths and the return of Christ at the end of the age. In the intermediate state, as we saw in chapter 3, the souls of believers are made perfect in holiness and go immediately into the presence of Christ (Phil. 1:23). To be sure, this condition is "far better" than our present condition of imperfectly sanctified souls united to perishing bodies (v. 23). But while it is "better," it is not "best." What is "best"—our ultimate or highest hope—is to dwell in the presence of Christ as whole persons, perfectly sanctified souls *and* resurrected bodies, forever reunited and inseparable.

Furthermore, the Bible tells us, what awaits us will be "a new heaven and a new earth, for the first heaven and the first earth had passed away, and the sea was no more" (Rev. 21:1). The hope of a *new* heaven and a *new* earth raises the question of the relationship of that new creation to the present creation. Will it be "an entirely new creation" or "a renewal of the present creation"?[1] Will God annihilate the old and replace it with something new, or will He transform the old into something new and better?

Scripture indicates that what awaits the present creation is transformation, not destruction. To be sure, Peter tells us that "the heavens will pass away with a roar, and the heavenly bodies will be burned up and dissolved, and the earth and the works that are done on it will be exposed. . . . The heavens will be set on fire and dissolved, and the heavenly bodies will melt as they burn!" (2 Peter 3:10, 12). But fire need not mean utter destruction. It may refer rather to purification or refinement (compare Ps. 12:6; Zech. 13:9; Mal. 3:3).

This understanding of refining finds confirmation in the way that Paul describes the future of the creation in Romans 8: "For the creation was subjected to futility, not willingly, but because of him who subjected it, in hope that the creation itself will be set free from its bondage to corruption and obtain the freedom of the glory of the children of God. For we know that the whole creation has been groaning together in the pains of childbirth until now" (vv. 20–22). The creation's destiny is not annihilation. Rather, it is freedom from its present bondage and entrance into the "freedom of the glory of the children of God." Thus, the creation now "groan[s] . . . in the pains of childbirth." Just as the delivery of a child follows labor pains, so the renewal and transformation of the creation will follow its present corrupted state.

In heaven, we will not be floating as disembodied souls among the clouds of the air. We will dwell in new heavens and a new earth as embodied souls. God will destroy neither our bodies nor the creation as a whole. He will renew and transform them. Each is a critical dimension of the Bible's teaching about heaven.

A State of Rest

Second, the Bible describes heaven as a state of rest. First, there is a rest from our present works: "'Blessed are the dead who die in the Lord from now on.' 'Blessed indeed,' says the Spirit, 'that they may rest from their labors, for their deeds follow them!'" (Rev. 14:13); "There remains a Sabbath rest for the people of God, for whoever has entered God's rest has also rested from his works as God did from his" (Heb. 4:9–10).[2] The "labors," "deeds," and "works" in view are the good works that God enables us to do in this life by grace.[3] These good works are frequently arduous and toilsome. Paul, for instance, encourages us: "And let us not grow weary of doing good, for in due season we will reap, if we do not give up. So then, as we have opportunity, let us do good to everyone, and especially to those who are of the household of faith" (Gal. 6:9–10; compare 2 Thess. 3:13). The world, the flesh, and the devil stand arrayed against us to keep us from doing good works. Paul can describe his own service to Christ as "toil" (Col. 1:29; 1 Thess. 2:9; 2 Thess. 3:8; 1 Tim. 4:10), and Jesus can describe the believer's service in such terms as well (see Rev. 2:2). To be sure, believers share in this rest immediately after they die and go to be with Christ. But only in heaven do they fully experience the blessedness of this rest, the refreshment that comes with the satisfying completion of our life's work and the final defeat of all of God's enemies.

Second, this rest is not an idle resting. Every picture of heaven that we have in Scripture is of a place that is teeming with activity.[4] In particular, the centerpiece of heaven is the worship of the triune God (see Rev. 4:1–5:14; 7:13–17; 22:3), a worship that takes place "day and night"—that is, ceaselessly (7:15).[5] That worship is not solitary or individualistic but corporate, undertaken as a redeemed assembly. Worship, in other words, is profoundly social. Other descriptions of heaven confirm that it will be a social and relational place. Heaven is described as a city, inhabited by the redeemed (21:22–26). Jesus describes heaven as a "marriage feast" (Matt. 22:2; 25:10; compare Rev. 19:9). We will live and worship God alongside one another. And in the bonds of that worship, we will know and love one another and serve and do good to one another.[6]

A State of Everlasting Rest

Third, heaven will be an everlasting rest.[7] What do we mean when we say that heaven will be eternal or everlasting? We do not mean to imply that we will be eternal in the way that God is eternal. We are creatures. We can never obtain or share in divine eternality. We will never cease to be creatures and will always live bounded by time. We also do not mean to say that we will be static or "motionless" in heaven.[8] Heaven, we have already seen, is a place that is full of activity. There we will know God, worship God, and love God and will also know and love our fellow saints and angels.

One important sense in which heaven may be said to be everlasting is that we will no longer experience the decay and corruption that is part of life in this fallen world. Our bodies are currently mortal and dying (2 Cor. 4:16). Spiritually, we are subject to decays of grace and backsliding (see Rev. 2:4–5a). But in heaven we will experience life to the full, with no possibility of decay or decline. Our bodies will be incorruptible, joined to souls that, by the grace of God, are incapable of sinning. This state of perfection will continue forever, without interruption. There is, moreover, no tension or contradiction between saying that heaven is "fixed" and saying that we can and will know God and love God to greater and greater degrees.[9] Our heavenly rest is active and, as such, admits of growth. In the worship of God, we will know God better and better, love Him more and more, and love our fellow saints and angels more and more. Part of the beauty of this everlasting rest is that, like the Israelite pilgrims of old, we will go "from strength to strength" (Ps. 84:7).

The Absence of Sin and Misery

Fourth, heaven is marked by the entire absence of sin and misery. This is evident from biblical descriptions of its inhabitants. There are the elect angels, who never fell into sin (compare 1 Tim. 5:21 with 2 Peter 2:4). And there are elect people, whose "deeds follow them" (Rev. 14:13). They carry only their good works with them into glory. The people of God as a whole appear before Christ "in splendor, without spot or wrinkle or any such thing, that [they] might be holy and without blemish" (Eph. 5:27). Note how the Bible describes the new Jerusalem—that is, the church triumphant in contrast with the wicked: "Blessed are those who wash their robes, so that they may have the right to the tree of life and that they may enter the city by the gates. Outside are the dogs and sorcerers and the sexually immoral and murderers and idolaters, and everyone who loves and practices falsehood" (Rev. 22:14–15). Sin is entirely excluded from heaven.

And because there is a complete absence of sin in heaven, there is equally a complete absence of misery in heaven. We read in Revelation that the inhabitants of heaven "shall hunger no more, neither thirst anymore; the sun shall not strike them, nor any scorching heat . . . , and God will wipe away every tear from their eyes" (Rev. 7:16–17); and again: "He will wipe away every tear from their eyes, and death shall be no more, neither shall there be mourning, nor crying, nor pain anymore, for the former things have passed away" (21:4). Because sin is absent from heaven, the misery that has flooded the world in the train of sin will be absent as well.

The Presence of Complete Joy

Fifth, heaven is not merely distinguished by what is absent from it. It is marked by the presence of complete joy. God has established an unbreakable link between holiness and happiness. This was true in the garden of Eden. Adam and Eve were happy so long as they continued in the holiness in which God had made them. In the kingdom of God, Paul reminds us, there is "righteousness and peace and joy in the Holy Spirit" (Rom. 14:17). The Holy Spirit is pleased to bring joy to sinners redeemed by Christ. What is true in part now will be true in full in heaven. As a place of complete holiness, it will equally be a place of complete joy.

How may we think of the joy of heaven? The Bible helps us think of that joy along two lines. In the first place, there is joy in the ingathering of heaven's residents, angels and human beings. One reason that we may say this with confidence is that the Bible tells us that there is supposed to be joy in the present assembly of believers. What should prompt that joy? It is witnessing the fruit of God's grace in the lives and service of one another. John told the churches, "I have no greater joy than to hear that my children are walking in the truth" (3 John 4). Paul told the Thessalonians: "For what is our hope or joy or crown of boasting before our Lord Jesus at his coming? Is it not you? For you are our glory and joy" (1 Thess. 2:19–20). If this is true both now and at the coming of Christ, surely it will continue in heaven. No small measure of our joy will stem from observing what God has accomplished in one another's lives.

But second, we have not yet reached to the highest, greatest joy of heaven. That, of course, stems from dwelling in the presence of our God (see Ps. 21:6). What makes heaven "heaven" is the presence of the triune God in His grace and mercy to His people: "Behold, the dwelling place of God is with man. He will dwell with them, and they will be his people, and God himself will be with them as their God" (Rev. 21:3). The great covenant principle—"I will be their God, and they shall be my people" (Jer. 31:33; compare Gen. 17:7; Ex. 6:7)— finds its fullest expression in heaven. We will know the supreme blessedness of dwelling in the presence of our Maker and Redeemer and beholding Him.

This sight of God has been called the *beatific vision*, or blessed vision. How may we describe this sight of God that is the centerpiece of our experience in heaven? In the first place, it is "immediate or direct"—that is, "without the need of [God's] being reflected either in nature or in Scripture."[10] This is what Paul tells the Corinthians: "For now we see in a mirror dimly, but then face to face. Now I know in part; then I shall know fully, even as I have been fully known" (1 Cor. 13:12). The Apostle John tells us, "Beloved, we are God's children now, and what we will be has not yet appeared; but we know that when he appears we shall be like him, because we shall see him as he is" (1 John 3:2). With a direct sight or vision of God, "we shall be like him." We will remain, of course, creatures. We are in no way introduced into the God-head; nor do we become gods. But as we behold God, we who are His image bearers will experience the full conformity of image bearers to their God. To see God, to know God, and to enjoy God—this "make[s] up the essence of our future blessedness."[11] "Without any hint of fear and shame," and "dwell[ing] in God's blessed presence," we will completely answer the purpose for which we were created and redeemed—to "glorify and enjoy him forever."[12]

What Does the Bible Teach about Hell?

An Embodied State

The Bible tells us correspondingly at least five things about hell. First, hell is an embodied state. The souls of the wicked, at the resurrection, will be forever reunited to their bodies. After the final judgment, they will be "thrown into the lake of fire"—that is, "the second death" (Rev. 20:15, 14). Hell experienced in eternity will be worse than hell experienced in the intermediate state, since both soul *and* body will undergo its torments. The whole person will be an object of the just judgment of God.

An Absence of Rest

In Isaiah, we read that turmoil and agitation characterize the sinful lives of the wicked (Isa. 57:20). And so, God declares, "there is no peace ... for the wicked" (57:21; 48:22). Hell will no less be marked by an absence of peace and of rest: "And the smoke of their torment goes up forever and ever, and they have no rest, day or night, these worshipers of the beast and its image, and whoever receives the mark of its name" (Rev. 14:11). There is no rest or respite from their just punishment, nor is there any refreshment in the midst of their torment (compare Luke 16:24–25).

An Everlasting Condition

Just as Jesus will bring the sheep into "eternal life," so He will cast the goats into "eternal punishment" (Matt. 25:46). The torments of the wicked will continue "forever and ever" (Rev. 14:11; compare Isa. 34:8, 10). Why are the punishments of hell endless and not limited in duration? Hell's torments are endless, in part, because the wicked have committed sins against God. Every sin, since it is against the infinite God, carries "infinite demerit" and therefore receives "a punishment infinite in duration."[13] Hell is also eternal because people do not stop sinning when they enter hell. And so *"endless* sin deserves *endless* punishment."[14] The endlessness of the punishments of hell is therefore entirely just.

The Presence of Sin and Misery

In this life, human beings enjoy the restraining influences of God's common grace. In hell, those restraints will be removed. Hell will be a world populated with wicked angels and sinners who will be left to sin without the checks or restraints of this life. The society of hell will make it even worse. As the devils now tempt people to sin and inflict misery on sinners, so they will compound the misery of hell's human residents. Human beings in hell will make themselves more and more miserable, since people in hell have no love for one another. Paul describes the ungodly to Titus in these terms: "hated by others and hating one another" (Titus 3:3a). This hatred will come to full expression in hell. It is a place marked by the presence of sin and all its attendant misery.

The Absence of Joy

Finally, there is no joy in hell. Because there is no holiness in hell, there is and can be no happiness. There is only misery and despair. We should not conclude, however, that since holiness and joy are absent from hell, God is Himself absent from hell. God is very much present in hell. He is present to the wicked angels and the reprobate in hell in His wrath and judgment (Rom. 2:5, 9; Rev. 14:9–11). The worst thing about hell is not what one will receive from the other people or devils who dwell there. The worst thing about hell is the presence of God in endless judgment, without a drop of mercy or even the hope of mercy. Every human being will spend eternity with God. In heaven, God will be present to His people as Father in love and joy; in hell, God will be present to sinners in righteous judgment and wrath.

Why Does the Bible Speak about Hell and Heaven?

Now that we have a sense of what the Bible teaches about heaven and hell, in one of which every person will reside, we may ask why the Bible reveals these things to us. What do future and perhaps far-off realities have to do with my day-to-day life? The Bible's answer is "everything."

Why Hell?

The Bible reveals hell to us for at least three reasons.[15] In the first place, the Bible's teaching about hell shows us the evil of sin and what sin truly deserves.[16] We live in a world that denies sin as sin, that excuses sin, that calls sin by the name of virtue, and that tries to mitigate sin and its seriousness. And of course, we often find our hearts doing the very same thing. We typically do not see our sin in its true light—as an offense against the just, holy, and righteous God. The doctrine of hell forces us to do that. It makes us see sin as the greatest evil that there is.

Second, the Bible's teaching about hell shows people their need to find refuge in Jesus Christ, without delay.[17] Of course, no sinner can ever, by the power of mere persuasion, be brought to break from his sin and to turn to

God. No soul has ever been scared into the kingdom of God. Even the punishments of sin cannot change the heart (see Rev. 16:10–11). This is true of the doctrine of hell. If the knowledge of hell cannot change the heart, cause one to break from sin, or bring one to love God in sincerity, then why does Scripture reveal it?

While the knowledge of hell is powerless in itself to change the heart or to bring a person to true repentance, it can bring the sinner to think about eternal realities that he might not otherwise consider. If he realizes that he deserves eternal punishment for his sins, then, if only from self-interest, he may seek out some refuge. The gospel reveals Christ as the only God-given refuge to sinners, and Christ is freely offered to sinners for their salvation. The sinner, awakened by the knowledge of his certain judgment and punishment and hearing what the gospel offers, may, by the sovereign grace and mercy of God, come to Jesus Christ in repentance and faith for salvation.

Third, the Bible's teaching about hell should prompt us to be thankful to Christ for enduring judgment on the cross.[18] The cross sets on display both the mercy *and* the justice of God (Rom. 3:26). Christ took the penalty for sin that sinners deserve, becoming a curse for them (see Gal. 3:10, 13). At Calvary, the sins of the elect were imputed to Him, and He made full satisfaction for those sins. At the cross, Christ bore the wrath of God that sinners deserve for their sins (Rom. 3:25 with 1:18). All this He did in self-giving love to His rebels and enemies (see Rom. 5:6–11; Gal. 2:20). It is because Christ at the cross fully satisfied the justice of God that I am no longer liable to eternal punishment for sin. Knowing what Christ did at the cross should stir me to thankfulness (compare Rev. 5:9, 11). The doctrine of hell, and its testimony to the justice of God in punishing sin, helps me appreciate, in love and wonder, the heights of Christ's love for me at the cross.

Why Heaven?

Finally, why does the Bible reveal heaven? There is one main reason: to help us in our pilgrimage on earth. Specifically, the hope of heaven encourages us to live lives of holiness in the here and now. John sets before us the hope that "when [Jesus] appears we shall be like him, because we shall see him as he is" (1 John 3:2). This hope should have a transformational effect on our lives right now: "And everyone who thus hopes in him purifies himself as he is pure" (v. 3). The hope of heaven is a purifying hope. Peter queries us, in light of the fiery transformation of the creation at the return of Christ (2 Peter 3:10), "What sort of people ought you to be in lives of holiness and godliness[?]" (v. 11) and urges us to "be diligent to be found by him without spot or blemish, and at peace" (v. 14).

Unbelief often vilifies the doctrine of heaven as escapist. It is calculated, critics say, to distract people from facing and dealing with the needs and problems of this life. Nothing could be further from the truth. God reveals heaven so that we may pursue holiness across the range of our present callings—as husbands and wives, parents and children, employers and employees, rulers and citizens, and friends and neighbors. Heaven is designed to transform our attitudes, thinking, and behavior in every arena and sphere of life.

For these reasons, the truly heavenly-minded person is one who currently "hunger[s] and thirst[s] for righteousness" (Matt. 5:6). It should be said of every Christian as it was said of Richard Sibbes: "Heaven was in him, before he was in heaven." Heaven is not merely a place or a destination (though it is that). It is a place characterized by the presence of the merciful and righteous triune God. It is where, seeing and knowing this God, we will fully glorify and enjoy Him. And that, of course, is the work that God has already started. Knowing God in Jesus Christ, we aim in everything to glorify and enjoy Him in this life (1 Cor. 10:31). Heaven will simply mark the finishing touches on God's handiwork (2 Cor. 3:18). And because God always finishes what He starts (see Phil. 1:6), we can give ourselves, entirely and without reservation, to the project of personal holiness, no small part of which involves serving our neighbors. The more that heaven is real and present to our thinking, the more we will want of Christ, and the more we will want to be conformed to Christ. And this is the very best way to live and to die: to draw nearer and nearer to the One who is life Himself!

Notes

Chapter 1

1   "Number of Original Scripted TV Series in the United States from 2009 to 2019," Statista, accessed January 19, 2021, https://www.statista.com/statistics/444870 /scripted-primetime-tv-series-number-usa/.
2   Pascal, *Pensées*, trans. A.J. Krailsheimer (London: Penguin, 1966), 66 (*Pensée* 169).
3   Pascal, 72 (*Pensée* 166).
4   Timothy A. Sisemore, *Finding God While Facing Death* (Fearn, Scotland: Christian Focus, 2017), 19.
5   Sisemore, 19.
6   Sisemore, 19.
7   "The Most Played Songs at Funerals Revealed—and Some Choices Are Bizarre," Smooth Radio, accessed January 19, 2021, https://www.smoothradio.com/news /quirky/most-popular-funeral-music-songs/.
8   Joel R. Beeke and Christopher W. Bogosh, *Dying and Death: Getting Rightly Prepared for the Inevitable* (Grand Rapids, Mich.: Reformation Heritage, 2018), 19.
9   The same would be true, of course, of Elijah, who was taken to heaven by a whirlwind, accompanied by "chariots of fire and horses of fire" (2 Kings 2:11).
10 We will take up the special case of Jesus Christ in later chapters. As a human being, Jesus died, but not for the same reasons that you and I will die. For one thing, we have no choice but to die. Jesus sovereignly chose to die.
11 From "The Sands of Time Are Sinking," Hymnary.org, accessed January 19, 2021, https://hymnary.org/text/the_sands_of_time_are_sinking. In the nineteenth century, Anne R. Cousin drafted this hymn by drawing together statements from across the *Letters* of the seventeenth-century Scottish Presbyterian pastor Samuel Rutherford.

Chapter 2

1   Here, we do not use the word *natural* to mean that God created human beings to die. Death is the result of sin, after all. But *natural* refers to death as relating to our nature—the temporary separation of a person's soul and body.
2   Before the resurrection, the wicked will suffer in hell in soul. After the resurrection and final judgment, the wicked's sufferings in hell will be in soul and body.
3   I have addressed these verses more fully in my *The Life and Theology of Paul* (Sanford, Fla.: Reformation Trust, 2018), 61–69.
4   The phrase "ordinary generation" is critical here. It refers to the fact that human beings descend from Adam, having been conceived through the (sexual) union of

their parents. There is one true human being who traces His descent from Adam, but not by "ordinary generation." That man, of course, is Jesus Christ, who was "conceived by the power of the Holy Ghost in the womb of the virgin Mary, of her substance, and born of her" (Westminster Larger Catechism 37). Thus, He was conceived and born "without sin" (WLC 37). Jesus is descended *from* Adam, but He is not *in* Adam because He is the *last* Adam, the second man (1 Cor. 15:45, 47).

5   The thought and reality of death can prompt genuine Christians to fear. In a later chapter, we will think about why that is, and how Christians can face those fears in faith.

6   William Bates, *The Whole Works of the Rev. W. Bates, D.D.*, ed. W. Farmer, 4 vols. (n.d.; repr., Harrisonburg, Va.: Sprinkle, 1990), 3:247.

7   Bates, 3:246. Bates notes that even Jesus shrank from death for this reason: "Our blessed Saviour, without the least impeachment of the rectitude and perfection of his nature, expressed an averseness from death, and with submission to the divine will desired a freedom from it. His affections were holy and human, and moved according to the quality of their objects" (3:246).

8   Bates, 3:249.

Chapter 3

1   The former has typically found a home in modern theological liberalism. The latter was advocated in the last century, arguably, by Karl Barth, on which see Oliver Crisp, "On Barth's Denial of Universalism," *Themelios* 29, no. 1 (2003): 18–29.

2   This way of thinking is reflected in the title (and argument) of Rob Bell's controversial book *Love Wins: A Book about Heaven, Hell, and the Fate of Every Person Who Ever Lived* (New York: HarperOne, 2012).

3   This is not to deny, of course, that Christ's return will mark the consummation of the salvation that God's people have already begun to experience in Christ.

4   Paul Helm, *The Last Things: Death, Judgment, Heaven and Hell* (Edinburgh, Scotland: Banner of Truth, 1989), 113.

5   Helm, *The Last Things*, 114–15. Helm rightly notes, however, that heaven no less magnifies the justice of God in that every redeemed inhabitant has been given entry through the blood of Christ, who paid the penalty for their sins on the cross. Because Christ has made *full* satisfaction for the sins of the redeemed, we may say that God's justice is most fully magnified in the saints in heaven.

6   For an older and technical, but still valuable, treatment of such views, see B.B. Warfield, "Annihilationism," in *The Works of Benjamin B. Warfield*, vol. 9, *Studies in Theology* (Oxford, England: Oxford University Press, 1932), 447–57.

7   To be sure, one must be careful in drawing points of doctrine from the parables that Jesus taught. The whole parable, however, assumes the reality of a future state of rewards and punishments for human beings who are now living. Without that assumption, we could make little sense of our Lord's teaching.

8   Louis Berkhof, *Systematic Theology*, new ed. (Grand Rapids, Mich.: Eerdmans, 1996), 691.

9   One way that He will consummate their salvation is by gloriously raising them from the dead.

10 *Catechism of the Catholic Church*, 2nd ed. (New York: Doubleday, 2003), §1030.

11 "Council of Trent: Decree on Purgatory," in *Compendium of Creeds, Definitions, and Declarations on Matters of Faith and Morals*, orig. comp. Heinrich Denzinger, eds. Peter Hünermann, Robert Fastiggi, and Anne Englund Nash, 43rd ed. (San Francisco: Ignatius, 2012), §1820.

12 "Council of Trent: Decree on Justification," in *Compendium*, §1580. The distinction between an eternal and temporal punishment for sin is a legitimate one in itself, but it has been profoundly misapplied here. The Bible teaches that Christ makes a complete, full, and sufficient satisfaction for the sins of His people such that there is no judicial barrier to any believer's entering heaven immediately upon his death.

Chapter 4

1 In the marvelous formulation of Westminster Confession 8.2: "The Son of God, the second person of the Trinity, being very and eternal God, of one substance and equal with the Father, did, when the fulness of time was come, take upon Him man's nature, with all the essential properties, and common infirmities thereof, yet without sin; being conceived by the power of the Holy Ghost, in the womb of the virgin Mary, of her substance. So that two whole, perfect, and distinct natures, the Godhead and the manhood, were inseparably joined together in one person, without conversion, composition, or confusion. Which person is very God, and very man, yet one Christ, the only Mediator between God and man."

2 In the words of the Westminster Shorter Catechism, Jesus, as to His humanity, had and still has a "true body" and a "reasonable soul" (WSC 22).

3 The New Testament speaks of union with Christ in eternity. We were chosen in Christ from before the foundation of the world (Eph. 1:4). The New Testament also speaks of union with Christ representatively. He died and rose again as our representative (Rom. 4:25; Gal. 3:13). But primarily the New Testament speaks of our union with Christ experientially—that is, when we are united with Christ in time, by the Holy Spirit and through faith.

4 The ESV reads, "Therefore, if anyone is in Christ, he is a new creation." That translation is not mistaken, but neither does it adequately convey what Paul is saying. The words "he is" are not present in the Greek text. Paul's point is that once a person has been savingly united to Christ, he has been introduced into "new creation." The "new creation" is not describing the believer, individually considered, so much as Christ and all that Christ has accomplished and secured for the believer.

5 The same Spirit by whose power Jesus' humanity was conceived in Mary's womb; the same Spirit who abode upon Christ to empower His ministry, beginning at His baptism; the same Spirit who raised Jesus from the dead; the same Spirit whom Jesus, with the Father, poured out in fullness on the day of Pentecost—this is the Spirit who indwells us now.

6 Sinclair B. Ferguson, *The Holy Spirit* (Downers Grove, Ill.: InterVarsity, 1996), 111.

7 This is not, however, to identify the Mosaic covenant with the covenant of works. Nor is it to say that God intended for the Mosaic covenant to be a republication of the covenant of works for Israel.

Chapter 5

1   The Bible also speaks of sin as a "debt" to God (Matt. 6:12; 18:32; Col. 2:14).

2   Johannes G. Vos, *The Westminster Larger Catechism: A Commentary*, ed. G.I. Williamson (Phillipsburg, N.J.: P&R, 2002), 197.

3   Vos, 197.

4   Vos, 198.

5   Vos, 198.

6   Vos, 198.

7   Keith Getty and Stuart Townend, "In Christ Alone" (2001).

8   A portion of this sermon has been reprinted in Nancy Guthrie, ed., *O Love That Will Not Let Me Go: Facing Death with Courageous Confidence in God* (Wheaton, Ill.: Crossway, 2011), 105–9. Luther preached this sermon in 1519.

9   William Perkins, *A Salve for a Sick Man, or a Treatise Containing the Nature, Differences, and Kinds of Death, as also the Right Manner of Dying Well*, in *The Works of William Perkins*, eds. Joel R. Beeke and Derek W.H. Thomas, 10 vols. (Grand Rapids, Mich.: Reformation Heritage, 2014–20), 10:446, 455.

10 Edward Pearse, *The Great Concern: Preparation for Death* (Grand Rapids, Mich.: Soli Deo Gloria, 2020), 15.

11 Thomas Boston, *Man's Fourfold State*, in *The Complete Works of the Late Rev. Thomas Boston, Ettrick*, ed. Samuel M'Millan, 12 vols. (London: William Tegg & Co., 1853), 8:267. The whole discussion on the death of the godly is found at 8:255–70. A portion of this discussion appears in Guthrie, *O Love That Will Not Let Me Go*, 111–18.

12 Pearse, *Great Concern*, 15.

13 As quoted in Perkins, *Salve for a Sick Man*, 10:450.

14 Guthrie, *O Love That Will Not Let Me Go*, 106.

15 Boston, *Man's Fourfold State*, 8:265.

16 To take two examples, Jonathan Edwards, "The Day of a Godly Man's Death Is Better Than the Day of His Birth," in *The Blessing of God: Previously Unpublished Sermons of Jonathan Edwards*, ed. Michael D. McMullen (Nashville, Tenn.: Broadman & Holman, 2003), 149–62; Thomas Boston, "The Improvement of Life in This World to the Raising a Good Name, the Best Balance for the Present, for the Vanity and Misery of Human Life; and the Good Man's Dying-Day Better than His Birth-Day," in *Works*, 5:461–501.

17 Thomas Brooks, *The Works of Thomas Brooks*, ed. Alexander B. Grosart, 6 vols. (1861–67; repr., Edinburgh, Scotland: Banner of Truth, 1980), 6:389–408.

18 Boston, *Man's Fourfold State*, 8:256.

Chapter 6

1   This conclusion finds confirmation in the context. In the immediately preceding verse, Paul tells the church, "Bless those who persecute you; bless and do not curse them" (Rom. 12:14). We may not limit, then, what Paul says in the following verse to Christians.

2   For an excellent, brief, biblical, and pastoral reflection on the Christian experience of grieving, see Donald Howard, *Christians Grieve Too* (Edinburgh, Scotland: Banner of Truth, 1980).

3   Compare Wilhelmus à Brakel's definition: "Hope is a propensity infused by God into the hearts of believers by means of the Word, whereby they patiently, actively, and with assurance anticipate future promised benefits." *The Christian's Reasonable Service*, trans. Bartel Elshout, 4 vols. (Pittsburgh: Soli Deo Gloria, 1992–95), 4:317.

4   The following examples have been drawn from Jeffrey A.D. Weima, *1–2 Thessalonians*, BECNT (Grand Rapids, Mich.: Baker, 2014), 315.

5   I have drawn inspiration for this approach to the passage from the Puritan Thomas Case, *Mount Pisgah; or, A Prospect of Heaven. Being an Exposition of 1 Thess. 4:13–18*, in *The Select Works of Thomas Case* (1836; repr., Ligonier, Pa.: Soli Deo Gloria, 1993). My outline, however, differs from that of Case.

6   It is possible to translate verse 14 thus: "God will bring with him those who have *fallen asleep through Jesus*." If so, Paul would be making the point that he makes in verse 16 in verse 14 also.

7   Paul is not saying declaratively that Jesus will certainly return in the lifetimes of his readers. He is saying, rather, that the return of Christ (the exact time of which has not been revealed to us, Matt. 24:36; 1 Thess. 5:3) is imminent—that is, it could happen at any moment. When it does happen, the sequence of events described by Paul will transpire.

Chapter 7

1   The brain, it must be remembered, is an organ of the human body. We must therefore distinguish the brain from the soul.

2   Brian Croft, *Visiting the Sick: Ministering God's Grace in Times of Illness* (Leominster, England: DayOne, 2008), 43. Croft's book is an excellent, biblical, brief, and accessible guide to serving those who are sick and dying.

3   In view here are fellow believers whom Paul enjoins the Galatian Christians to serve. But the principle has wider application than to believers only. As we saw in the previous chapter, Paul instructs us to "weep with those who weep" (Rom. 12:15).

4   In chapter 9, we will look more closely at some of the ethical issues that people must often address as they face the medical dimensions of death and dying.

5   The previous verse makes it clear that the "prayer of faith" is offered by the elders of the sick person, who has invited them to come and to "pray over him" (James 5:14).

6   Sinclair B. Ferguson, *Let's Study James* (Edinburgh, Scotland: Banner of Truth, 2018), 124–25.

7   Ferguson, 125.

8   J.A. Motyer, *The Message of James*, BST (Downers Grove, Ill.: InterVarsity, 1985), 200.

9   Magdalene died in 1542, four years before Luther's own death. This exchange is recorded in Theodore G. Tappert, ed., *Luther: Letters of Spiritual Counsel*, LCC 18 (Philadelphia: Westminster, 1955), 50–51.

10   As quoted in Robert Reymond, *John Calvin: His Life and Influence* (Fearn, Scotland: Christian Focus, 2004), 129.

11   I have drawn many of these ideas from the excellent discussion of this subject in Paul Tautges, *Comfort Those Who Grieve: Ministering God's Grace in Times of Loss* (Leominster, England: DayOne, 2009), 104–6. See especially his chart detailing a pattern of "sixteen-month bereavement care" (104–6).

12   Herman Bavinck has defined the unpardonable sin (the blasphemy against the
     Holy Spirit) in these terms: "A sin against the Gospel in its clearest revelation, . . .
     not in doubting or simply denying the truth, but in a denial which goes against the
     conviction of the intellect, against the enlightenment of the conscience, against
     the dictates of the heart; in a conscious, willful, and intentional imputation to the
     influence and working of Satan of that which is clearly recognized as God's work,
     . . . in a willful declaration that the Holy Ghost is the Spirit of the abyss, that truth
     is a lie, and that Christ is Satan himself." As quoted in Philip Graham Ryken, *Luke*,
     2 vols., Reformed Expository Commentary (Phillipsburg, N.J.: P&R, 2009), 1:653.
13   Jesus' death covers even the sins that we are not able to confess. The fact that a
     believer who commits suicide is unable to confess that sin does not mean that that
     sin is unpardonable. Christ is "able to save to the uttermost those who draw near to
     God through him, since he always lives to make intercession for them" (Heb. 7:25).

Chapter 8

1   Notice that the people of Israel were observing the Sabbath in the wilderness *before*
    they received the Ten Commandments at Sinai (see Ex. 16:25–26). This detail
    helps us see that the Sabbath is not unique to the Mosaic covenant. As an ordinance
    established at the creation for all human beings, it is not even unique to Israel.
2   The command, which is perpetual, is that one day in seven is reserved for worship
    and rest. The particular day, however, is subject to change. From the creation to the
    resurrection, it was the last day of the week (Saturday). From the resurrection until
    Christ's return, it is the first day of the week (Sunday).
3   This is not to deny that believers currently rest in Jesus Christ (see Matt. 11:28–30).
    But the rest in view in Hebrews is entirely future.
4   Edward Pearse, *The Great Concern: Preparation for Death* (Grand Rapids, Mich.:
    Soli Deo Gloria, 2020), 69.
5   Herman Ridderbos aptly terms "faith" the "mode of existence of the new life."
    Paul: An Outline of His Theology, trans. John R. De Witt (Grand Rapids, Mich.:
    Eerdmans, 1975), 231.
6   For example, "Christ is in you" (Rom. 8:10) and "life" (see 8:6, 10–11).
7   And, Paul reminds us, if this life pattern is not present in our lives, then we have no
    basis on which to say that we "belong" to Christ (Rom. 8:9b).
8   This is not to say that believers don't or shouldn't gather at other times for
    fellowship and mutual encouragement. It is to say that the writer is thinking of the
    "regular gathering of the local assembly for worship and fellowship." William L.
    Lane, *Hebrews 9–13*, Word Biblical Commentary 47B (Dallas: Word, 1991), 289.
    In light of the context of the New Testament's teaching more generally, we may say
    that the writer is thinking of the weekly gathering of believers to worship God on
    the Lord's Day.
9   Thomas Boston, *Man's Fourfold State*, in *The Complete Works of the Late
    Rev. Thomas Boston, Ettrick*, ed. Samuel M'Millan, 12 vols. (London: William Tegg
    & Co., 1853), 8:265. By "pest house," Boston means a house that is full of disease.
10 Given the parallel between the two Adams and their representative work (Rom.
    5:12–21) and the character of the "life" that Christ has won for us, it is likely that

if Adam had obeyed God, he would have entered a richer, heightened experience of life in fellowship with God than he had previously enjoyed.

Chapter 9

1   Compare here the testimony of the answer to Westminster Shorter Catechism 74, which summarizes the requirement of the eighth commandment ("You shall not steal," Ex. 20:15) in this way: "The eighth commandment requires the lawful procuring and furthering the wealth and outward estate of ourselves and others." God calls us to the lawful building of our own "wealth and outward estate." He also calls us to help others do the same. Building wealth is not a pretext for sinful self-indulgence. It is a precursor to serving others, not least through acts of generosity and giving.

2   I am paraphrasing the exposition of the sixth commandment at Westminster Shorter Catechism 68–69.

3   Three good books are Gilbert Meilaender, *Bioethics: A Primer for Christians*, 4th ed. (Grand Rapids, Mich.: Eerdmans, 2020); Bill Davis, *Departing in Peace: Biblical Decision-Making at the End of Life* (Phillipsburg, N.J.: P&R, 2017); David VanDrunen, *Bioethics and the Christian Life: A Guide to Making Difficult Decisions* (Wheaton, Ill.: Crossway, 2009). One need not agree with every argument or position in these books to benefit from the guidance they offer Christians on these difficult issues.

4   One might shy away from this option for fear of unduly burdening his loved ones. For a robust and compelling response to this concern, see Gilbert Meilaender, "I Want to Burden My Loved Ones," *First Things*, March 2010, accessed March 22, 2021, https://www.firstthings.com/article/2010/03/i-want-to-burden-my-loved-ones.

5   Davis, *Departing in Peace*, 52. Davis stresses that "God's Word forbids us *as private citizens* to take steps that intentionally end someone's life" (52, emphasis mine). In other words, for instance, God forbids us as individual citizens to do what He permits, under limited circumstances, the state to do in the interests of justice.

6   On differing but complementary definitions of *health*, see Lauris Christopher Kaldjian, "Concepts of Health, Ethics, and Communication in Shared Decision Making," *Communication & Medicine* 14, no. 1 (2017): 89–92. Kaldjian argues that health "depends on *physical* criteria (bodily and biomedical criteria) . . . on *psychosocial* criteria (mental, emotional, spiritual and social, including self-esteem and self-concept); . . . on the possession of *capacity* (being enabled to live an active life); and . . . on taking of *control* (demonstrating the self-control needed to enact healthy behaviors" (89, emphasis original). I am indebted to Drs. Elizabeth and Sam Hensley for pointing me to this instructive and helpful article.

7   Kaldjian, 89, 88.

8   On values and goals, see Kaldjian, 88–89.

9   I have been helped in formulating these questions by Kaldjian, 89. On weighing benefits and burdens, see Davis, *Departing in Peace*, 41.

10 Davis, *Departing in Peace*, 59. For a helpful and accessible discussion distinguishing this principle from suicide or physician-assisted suicide, see VanDrunen, *Bioethics and the Christian Life*, 195–212.

11 "To reject or withdraw treatment because of its burdens is still a refusal of treatment, not of life. From among the various lives still available to a suffering patient— some longer than others; some filled with more burdens than others—he chooses one life in particular." Meilaender, *Bioethics*, 87. Meilaender goes on to note the critical distinction between viewing an ailing person's life as "a burden not worth continuing" and assessing "treatment" as "either useless or excessively burdensome" and therefore to be "refused or withdrawn" (88). The former is always forbidden. The latter is permissible as long as, in so acting, we "still choose life" (88).

12 VanDrunen, *Bioethics*, 219.

13 For a fuller and more technical discussion of the questions and issues involved here, see David W. Jones, "To Bury or Burn? Toward an Ethic of Cremation," *Journal of the Evangelical Theological Society* 53, no. 2 (June 2010): 335–47, accessed March 22, 2021, https://media.thegospelcoalition.org/wp-content/uploads /2010/07/29181806/Jones-To-Bury-or-Burn_JETS.pdf.

Chapter 10

1 See, e.g., Job 19:25–27; Ps. 16:10; Dan. 12:2. For a recent and accessible discussion of the Old Testament's teaching about the bodily resurrection, see Gabriel N.E. Fluhrer, *Alive: How the Resurrection of Christ Changes Everything* (Sanford, Fla.: Reformation Trust, 2020), 51–69.

2 Paul's words in 1 Corinthians 15:12 by no means require the conclusion that these individuals denied Jesus' resurrection from the dead. His primary concern in this chapter is with the resurrection of the believer's body from the dead.

3 M.L. Soards, as quoted in David E. Garland, *1 Corinthians*, Baker Exegetical Commentary on the New Testament (Grand Rapids, Mich.: Eerdmans, 2003), 678.

4 Charles Hodge, *An Exposition of the First Epistle to the Corinthians* (New York: Robert Carter and Brothers, 1864), 309.

5 I owe this designation to Herman Ridderbos, *Paul: An Outline of His Theology*, trans. John R. De Witt (Grand Rapids, Mich.: Eerdmans, 1975), 540.

6 Ridderbos, 540. Ridderbos observes that "in verses 36–50 the quality of the resurrection body is first dealt with, and then, in verses 51ff., the manner in which the resurrection event takes place" (540).

7 I am indebted here to the insights of Richard B. Gaffin Jr., *Resurrection and Redemption: A Study in Paul's Soteriology*, 2nd ed. (Phillipsburg, N.J.: P&R, 1987), 34–36.

8 Hodge, *First Corinthians*, 321.

9 Paul's statement in verse 29 ("Otherwise, what do people mean by being baptized on behalf of the dead? If the dead are not raised at all, why are people baptized on their behalf?") has long puzzled commentators. Some have seen Paul as describing a practice in the church in Corinth but not necessarily approving of it. Others see Paul as describing the self-understanding of those who present themselves for baptism—spiritually "dead" in trespasses and sins. While no interpretation is without its difficulties, Paul's main point is clear. The Corinthians' own practice with respect to baptism testified against the denial of the bodily resurrection circulating among them.

10 Paul W. Barnett, *1 Corinthians*, Focus on the Bible (Fearn, Scotland: Christian Focus, 2000), 292.

11 Ridderbos, *Paul*, 544.

12 Elsewhere, Scripture tells us that the sounding of the trumpet will accompany the return of Christ in glory to judge the world. Therefore, the resurrection of all people from the dead will immediately precede the final judgment (see Matt. 24:31; 1 Thess. 4:16).

13 Garland, *1 Corinthians*, 747.

Chapter 11

1 Louis Berkhof, *Systematic Theology* (Grand Rapids, Mich.: Eerdmans, 1938), 731. Berkhof notes that the public character of the final judgment "will serve the purpose . . . of displaying before all rational creatures the declarative glory of God in a formal, forensic act, which magnifies on the one hand His holiness and righteousness, and on the other hand, His grace and mercy" (731).

2 Paul is brought to the Areopagus because of the Athenians' interest in "this new teaching . . . that you are presenting" (Acts 17:19). In the previous verse, Luke characterizes the content of Paul's teaching in terms of "Jesus and the resurrection" (v. 18). We therefore expect that Paul's address in verses 22–31 is a presentation of the gospel.

3 Helm, *The Last Things*, 59.

4 Helm, *The Last Things*, 59.

5 Some have argued that the elect angels will stand in judgment at the last day as well; see Cornelis P. Venema, *The Promise of the Future* (Edinburgh, Scotland: Banner of Truth, 2000), 401.

6 Venema, 400.

7 Venema, 398.

8 See here the especially helpful questions and answers at Westminster Larger Catechism 89–90.

9 I am paraphrasing here the question and answer given at Westminster Larger Catechism 150: "Are all transgressions of the law of God equally heinous in themselves, and in the sight of God?" The following question and answer (WLC 151) details four categories of "aggravations" that render sins more heinous: the "persons offending," the "parties offended," the "nature and quality of the offense," and various "circumstances" attending the sin. See especially the biblical passages offered in support of each category.

10 The following sentences summarize the teaching of Westminster Confession of Faith 33.3.

11 Venema, *Promise of the Future*, 414.

12 Robert L. Dabney, *Syllabus and Notes of the Course of Systematic and Polemic Theology*, 5th ed. (Richmond, Va.: Presbyterian Committee of Publication, n.d.), 683.

13 Dabney, 683.

14 Francis Turretin, *Institutes of Elenctic Theology*, ed. James T. Dennison Jr., trans. George M. Giger, 3 vols. (Phillipsburg, N.J.: P&R, 1992–97), 3:629.

15 Jonathan Edwards, *The Works of Jonathan Edwards*, ed. Edward Hickman, 2 vols. (repr., Edinburgh, Scotland: Banner of Truth, 1974), 2:902.

16 Edwards goes on to say that since there will be no envy in heaven, believers will not be envious when they see one another's different capacities for enjoying God. On the contrary, they will rejoice in the good of others, and that joy will, in turn, increase their own happiness. "And there shall be no such thing as envy in heaven, but perfect love shall reign through the whole society. Those who are not so high in glory as others, will not envy those that are higher, but they will have so great, and strong, and pure love to them, that they will rejoice in their superior happiness; their love to them will be such that they will rejoice that they are happier than themselves; so that instead of having a damp to their own happiness, it will add to it. They will see it to be fit that they that have been most eminent in works of righteousness should be most highly exalted in glory; and they will rejoice in having that done, that is fittest to be done." Edwards, 2:902.

17 Turretin, *Institutes*, 3:602.

18 I am following the argument of Turretin: "If it is asked here whether the sins of the pious equally as well as of the wicked will be revealed, we answer that the negative seems more probable to us" (*Institutes*, 3:602).

19 "The gratuitous mercy of God does not wish our sins to be remembered anymore, but casts them behind its back. Now what God has once wished to be covered in this life, he will not reveal in the other." Turretin, *Institutes*, 3:602.

20 "If their sins were to be made known, it would lead to the disgrace and confusion of the pious, from which they ought to be free. For Christ will return for this end, that he may be glorious in his saints and be admired in believers." Turretin, *Institutes*, 3:602.

Chapter 12

1 Louis Berkhof, *Systematic Theology* (Grand Rapids, Mich.: Eerdmans, 1938), 737.

2 In the context of the argument of Hebrews 4:1–10, the "rest" in view is entirely future. This is not to deny that believers currently enjoy rest in Jesus Christ (Matt. 11:28–30), but it is to say that this present rest is not in view in Hebrews 4:9.

3 See here Helm, *The Last Things*, 93–94.

4 See Jonathan Edwards, "Heaven Is a World of Love," in *The Works of Jonathan Edwards*, vol. 8, *Ethical Writings*, ed. Paul Ramsey (New Haven, Conn.: Yale University Press, 1989), 366–97. This sermon is available online at www.edwards.yale.edu.

5 This is not to say that gathered worship will be the only activity in heaven. The social descriptions of heaven in the Bible suggest that we will serve one another in settings outside gathered worship. But gathered worship will be the central activity in heaven.

6 For these reasons, there is every indication that believers will recognize one another in heaven. These kinds of relationships are impossible without mutual recognition. Furthermore, if Jesus was recognizably Himself in His resurrection body (Luke 24:39) and if His disciples could recognize Jesus after His resurrection (John 21:7), then surely we will recognize one another in heaven.

7   The Puritans used this phrase to describe heaven. See William Bates, "The Everlasting Rest of the Saints in Heaven," in *The Whole Works of the Rev. W. Bates, D.D.*, ed. W. Farmer, 4 vols. (n.d.; repr., Harrisonburg, Va.: Sprinkle, 1990), 3:3–111; and the often-reprinted Richard Baxter, *The Saint's Everlasting Rest, or, A Treatise on the Blessed State of the Saints in Their Enjoyment of God in Heaven.*

8   Helm, *The Last Things*, 93.

9   Helm, *The Last Things*, 88, 93.

10 Johannes G. Vos, *The Westminster Larger Catechism: A Commentary*, ed. G.I. Williamson (Phillipsburg, N.J.: P&R, 2002), 216.

11 Herman Bavinck, *Reformed Dogmatics*, vol. 4, *Holy Spirit, Church, and New Creation*, ed. John Bolt, trans. John Vriend (Grand Rapids, Mich.: Baker, 2008), 722, as referenced in Cornelis P. Venema, *The Promise of the Future* (Edinburgh, Scotland: Banner of Truth, 2000), 482.

12 Venema, *Promise of the Future*, 488.

13 Turretin, *Institutes*, 3:607.

14 A.A. Hodge, *Outlines of Theology* (1879; repr., Edinburgh, Scotland: Banner of Truth, 1972), 584. Compare Turretin: "As he will never cease to sin against God, so neither to be punished by him." *Institutes*, 3:607.

15 For each of these, I am indebted to the discussion of William Bates, "The Four Last Things," in *Works*, 3:500–507.

16 See Bates, 3:502–4.

17 See Bates, 3:504–6.

18 See Bates, 3:506–7.

Subject Index

Abraham, 85, 90
Adam
  body of, 107
  creation of, 8
  curse of, 10
  disobedience of, 37
  fall of, 9, 14, 86
  as representative, 17
Ahithophel, 76
angels, 115, 117, 141
anger, 77
annihilation, 26–27, 124
assurance, 83
atonement, 38

backsliding, 126
Barth, Karl, 134
Bates, William, 20, 134
Bavinck, Herman, 138
beatific vision, 128
being there, 68–70
Berkhof, Louis, 141
biological death, 13, 15
Boccelli, Andrea, 5
body
  in heaven, 123
  as perishable, 107
  resurrection of, 62, 110
  and soul, 20–21, 68
  and union with Christ, 30–31
Boston, Thomas, 5, 49, 52, 53, 86, 138
Brakel, Wilhelmus à, 137
Brooks, Thomas, 53
Bunyan, John, 73
burials, 96–98

Calvin, John, 3, 51, 74
Cassidy, Eva, 5
Catechism of the Catholic Church, 28
celebrations of life, 5
Christian life, 105
church, 5–7
church history, 3
comfort, 61, 77, 83, 96, 116
condemnation, 39, 105
conscience, 49, 97, 116
consumerism, 5–6
corruption, 10, 87
Council of Florence (1431–49), 28
Council of Trent (1545–63), 28–29
covenant of works, 135
COVID-19 pandemic, 19
creation, and death, 7–8
cremation, 97
Croft, Brian, 137
culture, challenges from, 4–5

David, 58, 90
Davis, Bill, 139
deacons, 75
death
  certainty of, 16–19, 95
  and creation, 7–8
  dimensions of, 13–15
  encountering of, 57–60
  fear of, 19–21, 22, 48–52
  as last enemy, 11
  as penalty for sin, 8–9, 21, 133
  as state or condition, 45
  thinking more about, 52–53
  as universal in scope, 9, 10

145

victory over, 40
what happens after, 30–31
death penalty, 17
decay, 110, 126
deceased, speaking of, 76
denial, 4
despair, 41, 59
destruction, 124
dignity, 70, 96
disobedience, 14
distraction, culture of, 4
divine sovereignty, 26
division, 6, 119
Dorcas, 58
dying, ministering to, 67–75

Edwards, Jonathan, 120, 142
eighth commandment, 139
elders, 75
elect, 30–31
Elihu, 13–14
Elijah, 71–72, 133
encouragement, 61, 138
end-of-life decisions, 93–96
Enoch, 9
entertainment mentality, 6
envy, 142
escapism, 132
estate planning, 92–93
eternal death, 13, 15
eternal life, 7, 26–27, 38, 80
eternal punishment, 26–27, 129. *See also* hell
euthanasia, 95
evangelism, 32
Eve, 14
everlasting rest, 126
exiles, 85

fairness, 19
faith, 35–36, 40, 82
false teaching, 102, 105
fear
    of death, 19–21, 22
    facing of, 48–52

of final judgment, 121–22
of loss, 50–51
of pain, 51–52
of readiness, 49–50
feeding tubes, 96
fellowship, 84–85, 87, 138
Ferguson, Sinclair, 71–72
final judgment
    basic questions about, 115–17
    as essential to the gospel, 113–15
    facing of, 118–20
    fear of, 121–22
    of wicked and righteous, 117–18
finances, 92
firstfruits, 104
flesh, 106
foolishness, 106
Franklin, Benjamin, 16
funerals, 96–98

garden of Eden, 8, 14–15, 18, 38, 86, 127
God
    attributes of, 25
    decree of, 50
    justice of, 16–17, 18, 44, 63, 114, 131
    love of, 25, 46
    presence of, 88, 128
godliness, 119
good works, 118, 120
gospel, 21, 24, 31, 49–50, 58, 64, 73, 97
grace, 79–81, 126
gratitude, 76
grief, 57–61, 75–76
guilt, 77

happiness, 23, 127, 142
heaven
    as embodied state, 123–25
    recognition in, 142
    thinking often of, 86–88
hell
    as embodied state, 128–29
    immediacy of, 31, 63
    in Scripture, 130–31
    as "second death," 11, 15, 27

sin and misery in, 129–30
Helm, Paul, 26, 134
holiness, 119, 122, 127, 131
Holy Spirit
    blasphemy against, 138
    as bond of union with Christ, 35–36
    indwelling of, 82–83
    joy in, 127
    keeping in step with, 40
hope, 59–60, 97, 110, 132, 137
hospitals, 5
hymns, 69

image of God, 7, 128
imputation, 22, 37
infant mortality, 5
inheritance, 87
intermediate state, 23, 123–24
irrationality, 106
Isaac, 85, 90

Jacob, 57–58, 85, 90
Jesus Christ
    as Author of life, 11
    communion with, 47, 81–83
    death of, 22, 33–34, 114, 131
    Farewell Discourse of, 90
    humanity of, 34–35
    obedience of, 18
    pointing to, 72–74
    resurrection of, 37–38, 61, 103–6
    return of, 27, 28, 62–63, 86, 115–16,
        137
Job, 68–69, 71, 72
Joseph, 57–58
Joshua, 90
joy, 23, 127–28, 130
Judas Iscariot, 76
judgment, 25, 31, 113–15. *See also* final
    judgment
justification, 29, 37, 44, 73

Kaldjian, Lauris Christopher, 139

law, 89, 116

Lazarus, 58
letting die, 96
life, 82
living wills, 94
Lord's Day, 79–80, 84, 138
loss, 50–51, 87
Luther, Martin, 3, 48, 72

Martha, 58
martyrdom, 90
Mary (sister of Martha), 58
means of grace, 79–81
medical prognosis, 70–72
medicine, 95
Meilaender, Gilbert, 140
mental decline, 68
mental illness, 77
mercy, 19, 27, 114, 121, 131
miraculous healing, 70–72
misery, absence of, 126–27
missions, 32
mortality, 7
Mosaic covenant, 135, 138
Moses, 90
mourning, 75–76, 127
music, 4
mystery, 109

natural body, 107
natural death, 13, 14
neighbor, 93
new creation, 86, 124, 135
new heavens and new earth, 124
nursing homes, 5

obedience, 18
optimism, 23
ordinary generation, 133–34
orphans, 50–51, 74
Owen, John, 5, 43

paganism, 57, 60
pain, 51–52, 74
palliative care, 70, 96
parable of Lazarus and the rich man, 26

parable of the minas, 120
parable of the sheep and the goats, 25
paradox, 43
Pascal, Blaise, 4
peace, 23
Pearse, Edward, 48, 81
Perkins, William, 48, 51
physician-assisted suicide, 139
pilgrimage, 131
Pilgrim's Progress, 73
possessions, 92–93
power of attorney, 94
prayer, 69, 74–75
preaching, 6, 81
preparing
    for end of life, 65, 93–96
    of family and friends, 67–68, 90–92
    for funeral and burial, 96–98
    of worldly estate, 92–93
presence, 68–76
prognosis, 70–72
property, 92
propitiation, 35, 38, 44
punishment, degrees of, 27
purgatory, 28–30
Puritans, 52–53

readiness, fear of, 49–50
rebellion, 14, 24, 25, 85–86
reconciliation, 24, 31–32, 91–92, 119
Reformation, 3, 48
repentance, 28
representative relationship, 17–18
resentment, 77
rest, 125–26, 129, 142
resurrection
    bodies of, 107–8, 62, 101
    denial of, 102, 103
    firstfruits of, 104
    and the gospel, 103, 110
    hope of, 97, 110
    and union with Christ, 61
    victory of, 109–10
reunions, 62–63
rewards, 27, 119–20

Ridderbos, Herman, 138, 140
righteous, judgment of, 117–18
righteousness, imputation of, 22, 37
Roman Catholic Church, 28–30

Sabbath, 79–80, 125, 138
sacrifice, 37
salvation, 24, 32
Satan, 20, 41, 48, 49, 50
Saul, 76
Scripture
    on death, 9, 67, 90
    on heaven and hell, 29–30, 130–32
    reading of, 40, 69
second death, 11, 15, 27
second probation, 27–28
self-indulgence, 105, 139
selfishness, 77
sentimentality, 5
shame, 77, 108, 122
Sibbes, Richard, 132
sin
    absence of, 126–27
    account of, 121
    death as penalty for, 8–9, 21
    as indwelling, 47
    as sting of death, 109
Sinatra, Frank, 5
sixth commandment, 76, 93, 95, 96, 139
skepticism, 106
social media, 4
Solomon, 13, 90
soul, 20–21, 30, 68, 123
spiritual body, 107, 123
spiritual death, 13, 14, 15
sports, 4
stoicism, 58
strangers, 85
substance abuse, 77
suffering, 68–69, 91, 101
suicide, 76–77, 95, 139

television, 4
temptation, 41, 48
Ten Commandments, 89, 138

theological liberalism, 134
total depravity, 24
transformation, 88, 124, 131
trials, 27, 51, 71, 101
Turretin, Francis, 142

unbelief, 41, 59, 63–64, 132
uncertainty, 87
union with Christ, 34–36, 61, 81, 83,
    104, 135
universalism, 23–26
unpardonable sin, 77, 138

vanity, 110
ventilators, 96
victory, 11, 40
Vos, Johannes, 47

Wardlaw, Ralph, 60
weakness, 107

wealth, 139
weeping, 11, 58, 137. *See also* grief;
    mourning
Western culture, 3
Westminster Confession of Faith, 17,
    29–30, 34, 135
Westminster Larger Catechism, 30, 31,
    43, 44, 45, 134, 141
Westminster Shorter Catechism, 135,
    139
wicked
    annihilation of, 26–27
    judgment of, 115, 117–18
    punishment of, 31, 127, 129–30
    resurrection bodies of, 108, 128–29
widows, 50–51, 74
wilderness, 80, 138
Word of God, 81
world, 85–86
worship, 80–81, 84, 125, 142

Scripture Index

Genesis
1–2	8
1–3	7, 13
1:1	7
1:1b	7
1:20–21	7
1:22	7
1:24	7
1:26	7
1:28	8
1:31	8
2:2b–3	80
2:3	87
2:7	8
2:15–16	14
2:16	86
2:16–17	8
2:25	107
3:7	14, 107
3:8a	14
3:8b	15
3:17–18	10
3:19	9, 14
5:5	9
5:24	9
17:7	128
37	57
42:36	58
43:14	58
48:1–22	90

Exodus
6:7	128
16:25–26	138
20:8–11	80
20:13	76, 93, 95
20:15	139

Leviticus
18:5	38

Deuteronomy
5:12--15	80
10:18	50, 74
11:16–17	72
21:22–23	18
28:15	72
28:23	72
33:27	52

Joshua
24:1–28	90
24:15	91

1 Samuel
3:18	72

2 Samuel
1	58
12:21–23	30

1 Kings
2:1–9	90

Job
1:6–12	71
1:21	20, 92
13:4–5	69
2:1–6	71
2:12	68
2:13	69
34:14–15	13–14
42:7–9	69

Psalms
7:11	24
12:6	124
14:1–3	24
16:11	30
17:15	88
21:6	128
23	69
23:4	40
49:17	20
51:5	24
68:5	50, 74
84:7	126
90:3	16
90:12	16
116:15	47
130:3	19
139:16	16
146:9	50

Proverbs
11:14	96
15:22	96
24:6	96

Ecclesiastes
1:2	59
3:20	59
7:1	53
7:2	21
7:10	7

9:2	51	10:15	117	16:24	26, 31
12:7	13	10:28	15	16:24–25	129
		10:32	117	17:10	120
Isaiah		11:22	117	19:11–27	120
25:8	109	11:24	117	21:28	121
33:17	88	11:28–30	138, 142	21:34	86, 119
34:8	129	12:31	77	23:43	47
34:10	129	13:41–41	117	23:47	33
38:17	121	13:49–50	117	24:1	80
48:22	129	18:32	136	24:39	107, 142
51:11	11	22:2	125	24:42	107
52:13–53:12	37	24:31	117, 141	24:43	107
53:6	37	24:31–32	117		
57:1–2	31	24:36	115–16, 137	**John**	
57:20	129	24:42	119	3:16	46
57:21	129	24:44	119	3:36	25
		25:10	125	4:34	36
Jeremiah		25:31–33	63	5:22	63, 116
10:10	91	25:31–46	25	5:28–29	115
10:23	76	25:32	115	5:29	108
31:33	128	25:33	28, 117	6:37	50
		25:34	117	8:46	33
Daniel		25:35–36	118	11	58
12:2	15, 31, 108	25:41	28	11:25–26	101
		25:42–43	117	14–16	90
Hosea		25:46	15, 25, 26, 28	14:1	90
13:14	46, 109	28:1	80	14:1–3	32
				14:2	53
Jonah		**Mark**		14:6	24
2:9	49	12:30–31	89	15:1–17	120
		16:2	80	16:33	85
Micah				17:4	36
7:19	121	**Luke**		17:16	85
		1:35	33, 34	19:11	117
Zechariah		6:35	119	20:1	80
13:9	124	12:10	77	20:19	80
		12:20	16	20:26	80
Malachi		12:47	27	21:7	142
3:3	124	12:48	27, 117		
		13:2	28	**Acts**	
Matthew		13:3	28	3:15	11
5:6	132	13:4	28	3:20b–21	30
5:23–24	91	13:5	28	4:12	25
6:12	136	16:19–31	26	6:1–7	51
6:19–20	87	16:22	47	9:36–43	51

9:39	58	5:12b	9	13:11	84
16:28	77	5:17	22, 29, 38,	14:1–15:7	102
17:18	141		83, 120	14:12	117
17:19	141	5:18	38	14:17	127
17:22–31	141	5:19a	37	15:13	60
17:31	114, 116	5:19b	37		
17:32	102	5:21	22	**1 Corinthians**	
20:7	80	6:6–7	47	2:3	70
20:17–38	90	6:11	47	3:10–15	119
20:32	90	6:13a	111	3:21–22	40
24:15	108	6:14	47	6:3	115
24:25	114	6:23	9, 15, 27,	6:17	35
			44, 86	6:19–20	36
Romans		7:17	47	6:20	111
1:18	24, 37, 131	7:24	47	7:29	86
1:18–32	116	8	69	7:31	86
1:20–21	25	8:1	22, 39, 114	9:27	32
1:32	26	8:1–2	35	10:31	132
2:5	24, 130	8:1–11	64, 82, 83	12:12–13	84
2:9	130	8:3	34	13:12	128
2:11	118	8:4	40, 83	15	18, 39
2:12–16	114	8:5	40	15:1	102, 103
2:14	116	8:6	138	15:1–2	103
2:15	116	8:9	35, 82	15:1–3	37
2:15–16	117	8:9b	138	15:1–11	102, 103
2:16	114	8:10	35, 39, 82, 138	15:3	103
3:1	116	8:10–11	138	15:3–4	103
3:4	49	8:11	39, 82, 83	15:4	103
3:11–12	24	8:20–21	85	15:5–8	103
3:19	117	8:20–22	10, 124	15:10	110
3:21–26	22	8:23	31	15:12	102, 103,
3:21–26	37	8:28	46		140
3:23	107	8:32	46	15:12–19	104
3:24	37	8:33–34	114	15:12–34	102,
3:25	37, 131	8:34	39		103–5
3:26	131	9:14–15	49	15:13	104
4:5	49	9:18	63	15:14	104, 109
4:7–8	37	9:20–21	17	15:15	104, 105
4:25	37, 39, 105, 135	10:14–17	32	15:16	104
5:2	60	10:5	38	15:17	37, 104, 105
5:6	49	11:5–6	49	15:18	105
5:6–11	131	12:2	40, 52, 88	15:19	105
5:9–10	37	12:14	136	15:20	104, 105
5:12–21	18, 24, 82,	12:15	58, 137	15:22	16, 24, 35, 104
	86, 138	12:18	92	15:23	104, 105

15:24	105	16:22	84, 121	2:4–10	39, 87	
15:24–28	105			2:6	101	
15:25	105	**2 Corinthians**		2:8	19, 36	
15:26	11, 105	3:17	38	2:12	59	
15:27	105	3:18	47, 132	3:17	35–36	
15:29–34	105	4:16	68, 83, 126	4:23	40, 88	
15:30–31	105, 110	5:3–4	21	4:29	68	
15:32	105	5:6	30	5:25–27	36	
15:35	102, 106	5:7	40, 45, 61, 82	5:27	126	
15:35–41	106	5:8	26, 30	6:13	40	
15:35–49	102, 106–8	5:10	28, 115, 118, 121	6:14	40	
				6:17	40	
15:36	106	5:17	35, 82			
15:37	106	5:20	31	**Philippians**		
15:38	106	5:21	18, 29, 32, 33, 37	1:6	83, 132	
15:39–40a	106			1:21	22, 52, 81, 87	
15:40b–41	107	6:2	25	1:23	26, 30, 46, 47, 61, 124	
15:42	107	12:9	107			
15:42–43	123	13:4	107	1:29	19, 36	
15:42–44	39			2:7	34	
15:42–45	108	**Galatians**		2:8	36	
15:42–49	106, 107	2:16	29, 82	3:10	91	
15:43	107	2:20	36, 40, 61, 81, 82, 83, 131	3:20	85, 86	
15:43a	107			3:21	107	
15:44a	107	3:10	18, 131	3:21	39, 83	
15:44b–45a	107	3:12	38	4:7	74	
15:45	134	3:13	18, 114, 131, 135			
15:45	38			**Colossians**		
15:45b	107	3:14	82	1:29	125	
15:47	108, 134	4:4	34	2:13	14, 38–39	
15:47–48	107	5:18	40	2:14	38, 136	
15:49	108	5:22–23	64	2:15	38	
15:50	102	5:24	82	3:1	101	
15:50–58	102, 109–10	5:25	40, 83	3:3	68	
		6:2	69	3:4	38	
15:51	62, 109	6:9–10	125			
15:52	109, 111	6:14	82, 85	**1 Thessalonians**		
15:54	111, 123			2:9	125	
15:54b–55	109	**Ephesians**		2:19–20	128	
15:55–57	46, 102	1:3	36	4:13	57, 58, 60	
15:56	109	1:4	135	4:13–18	57, 60	
15:56–57	40	1:10	86	4:14	61, 62	
15:57	109	2:1	14, 21, 24	4:14–17	61	
15:58	102, 109, 110	2:1–2	14	4:16	31, 62, 141	
16:2	80	2:3	14	4:17	62	

4:18	61	4:9–10	125	2:24	37
5:2–3	20	4:10	80, 87		
5:3	137	4:11	80	**2 Peter**	
		6:19–20a	60	2:4	126
2 Thessalonians		7:25	138	3:10	124, 132
1:5–12	25	7:26	33	3:11	119, 132
1:8	25	9:11–28	37	3:12	124
1:9	27	9:27	9, 16, 28	3:14	119, 132
3:8	125	9:28	28		
3:13	125	10:24	84	**1 John**	
		10:24–25	84	1:2	43
1 Timothy		10:31	21	1:8–10	40
3:16	37	11:3	7	2:2	37
4:3–4	85	11:8–10	32	2:16–17	85
4:10	125	11:13	85	3:2	128, 131
5:1–16	51	11:13–16	32	3:3	132
5:6	14	11:16	85	4:19	98
5:8	93	12:14	122	5:4	85
5:21	126	12:22	88	5:12	25, 35
		12:22–23	87		
2 Timothy		12:23	30, 47	**3 John**	
1:8	91	12:24	88	4	127
1:10	11, 38	12:26–27	86		
1:12	91	12:28	86, 87	**Jude**	
3:16	82	13:14	87	6	31, 115
4:8	119, 121				
		James		**Revelation**	
Titus		1:2–4	71	1:10	80
2:13–14	60	2:14–26	118	2:2	125
3:3a	130	4:13	71	2:4–5a	126
		4:13–15	16	4:1–5:14	125
Hebrews		4:14–15	71	5:9	24, 131
2:9	11	5:11	71	5:11	131
2:14	11, 20	5:15	70, 71	6:911	26
2:14–15	38	5:16–18	71	7:13–17	125
2:15	20, 45			7:15	125
2:16–17	35			7:16–17	127
2:17	38	**1 Peter**		7:17	11
3:7–4:13	84	1:3	60	12:10	49
3:13	80	1:4	87	14:9-11	25, 130
4:1	87	1:4–5	87	14:11	27, 129
4:1–2	80	1:8	47	14:13	28, 30, 48, 87,
4:2–3	80	1:9	84		125, 126
4:4	87	1:17	118	16:10–11	15, 131
4:9	80, 87, 142	2:12	118	19:9	125
		2:15	118		

20:6	15	20:15	129	22:14–15	127
20:10	15	21:1	124	22:3	125
20:11–15	115	21:3	128	22:3–4	88
20:14	11, 15, 27,	21:4	127		
	101, 129	21:22–26	125		

About the Author

Dr. Guy Prentiss Waters is the James M. Baird Jr. Professor of New Testament at Reformed Theological Seminary in Jackson, Miss. Before joining the RTS faculty in 2007, Dr. Waters served as assistant professor of biblical studies at Belhaven University in Jackson. Dr. Waters is a graduate of the University of Pennsylvania (B.A.), Westminster Theological Seminary (M.Div.), and Duke University (Ph.D.). He is a teaching elder in the Presbytery of the Mississippi Valley of the Presbyterian Church in America. He is author or editor of several books, including *The Life and Theology of Paul, How Jesus Runs the Church, Justification and the New Perspectives on Paul,* and *The Federal Vision and Covenant Theology,* and he has written dozens of chapters, articles, and reviews.